Advanced Chi Nei Tsang

Enhancing Chi Energy in the Vital Organs

Mantak Chia

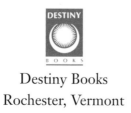

Destiny Books

Rochester, Vermont

Destiny Books
One Park Street
Rochester, Vermont 05767
www.DestinyBooks.com

Destiny Books is a division of Inner Traditions International

Library of Congress Cataloging-in-Publication Data
Chia, Mantak, 1944–
  [Chi Nei Tsang II]
  Advanced Chi Nei Tsang : enhancing chi energy in the vital organs / Mantak Chia.
     p. cm.
  Originally published: Chi Nei Tsang II. Chang Mai, Thailand : Universal Tao
Publications, 2000.
  Includes index.
  ISBN 978-1-59477-055-5 (pbk.)
  1. Qi gong. I. Title.
  RM727.C54M362 2007
  613.7'1489—dc22
                                                                    2009006516

Printed and bound in India by Replika Press Pvt. Ltd.

10 9 8 7 6 5 4 3 2 1

Text design and layout by Priscilla Baker
This book was typeset in Janson, with Futura and Present used as display typefaces

Contents

Acknowledgments

We extend our gratitude to the many generations of Taoist masters who have passed on their special lineage, in the form of an unbroken oral transmission, over thousands of years. We wish to especially thank Taoist Master Yi Eng for his patience and openness in transmitting the formulas of Taoist Inner Alchemy. We also wish to thank the thousands of unknown men and women of the Chinese healing arts who developed many of the methods and ideas presented in this book.

We offer our eternal gratitude to our parents and teachers for their many gifts to us. Remembering them brings joy and satisfaction to our continued efforts in presenting the Universal Tao System. As always, their contribution has been crucial in presenting the concepts and techniques of the Universal Tao.

We thank the many contributors essential to this book's final form: The editorial and production staff at Inner Traditions/Destiny Books for their efforts to clarify the text and produce a handsome new edition of the book and Victoria Sant'Ambrogio for her line edit of the new edition.

We wish to thank the following people for their assistance in producing the original edition of this book: Claire Spector for transcribing and editing the first draft of the manuscript; Marga Vianu, Annette Derksen, Sarina Stone, and Colin Campbell for preparing, editing, and proofreading the first draft; Chong Mi Mueller for her many good suggestions; and Dr. Angela Wu and Gilles Marin for their input in the process of transcribing the practice into manuscript form.

A special thank you goes to our Thai Production Team: Raruen

Keawpadung, Computer Graphics; Saysunee Yongyod, Photographer; Udon Jandee, Illustrator; and Saniem Chaisarn, Production Designer.

Finally, we wish to thank our certified instructors, students, and sponsors throughout the world for their ongoing contributions to the system and for preserving the vitality of the Universal Tao practices.

Putting Advanced Chi Nei Tsang into Practice

The practices described in this book have been used successfully for thousands of years by Taoists trained by personal instruction. Readers should not undertake these practices without receiving personal transmission and training from a certified instructor of the Universal Tao, since some of these practices, if done improperly, may cause injury or result in health problems. This book is intended to supplement individual training by the Universal Tao System and to serve as a reference guide for these practices. Anyone who undertakes these practices on the basis of this book alone does so entirely at his or her own risk.

The meditations, practices, and techniques described herein are not intended to be used as an alternative or substitute for professional medical treatment and care. If any readers are suffering from illnesses based on mental or emotional disorders, an appropriate professional health care practitioner or therapist should be consulted. Such problems should be corrected before training begins.

Neither the Universal Tao nor its staff and instructors can be responsible for the consequences of any practice or misuse of the information contained in this book. If the reader undertakes any exercise without strictly following the instructions, notes, and warnings, the responsibility must lie solely with the reader.

This book does not attempt to give any medical diagnosis, treatment, prescription, or remedial recommendation whatsoever, in relation to any human disease, ailment, suffering, or physical condition.

 # Introduction

Advanced Chi Nei Tsang is one of the most profound therapeutic massage forms found in classical Chinese and Thai medicine. Chi Nei Tsang practitioners assist those they work with in maintaining their health through tissue and organ massage and wind release techniques. It is essentially a facilitated form of self-care, since the highest form of its practice is teaching people to maintain their health and optimize their energy. The final goal is to allow people to set themselves free—physically, mentally, emotionally, and spiritually.

Negative and sick energies affect the physical body. The greater part of all disciplines of Chinese and Thai medicine involves treatments for neutralizing the destructive power of these sick and destructive energies. If properly addressed, the destructive impact of these immaterial and invisible wind forces can be avoided and considerable harm prevented. Another important part of the procedure is to teach students to sense and release the winds by themselves through healing exercises, meditations, and self-massage techniques.

The highly effective Advanced Chi Nei Tsang techniques for mastering the winds are the subject of this book. This advanced practice deals with the winds in the body, their blockages, and the ways to release them. Using these techniques, we are able to assist students with chronic and acute challenges in internal tissues, organs, and energy systems, improving and restoring their health. The procedures presented here build on the information and techniques contained in the first Chi Nei Tsang book; we assume that you have already integrated that information. This book is not a substitute for training from a qualified Chi Nei Tsang instructor.

Most of the work in Chi Nei Tsang is done on the abdominal area. The navel is a particularly intimate and important place. At conception, the first cell of the body is formed in the umbilicus, and every part of the body evolves in a spiral around this first cell. The navel is connected directly to every other part of the body; by working on the navel we can affect the whole body.

Those internal organs that are gathered in the abdominal area are protected by a cage of bones formed by the pelvis and the ribs. Emotions and wind accumulate in this area, and when it is congested and full of gas, all the natural functions of the body are impaired.

Trapped wind is heavy, gray, and sick, like a damp room with no ventilation. Using Advanced Chi Nei Tsang is akin to opening the right windows to let the stagnant wind go out and to assist in reestablishing a healthy flow of vital energy. When successful, Advanced Chi Nei Tsang can help energy to flow freely again.

The treatment always begins with the procedures included in the first Chi Nei Tsang book. Once the knots and tangles in the abdomen have been released and the organs have been detoxified over one or several sessions, you can just work on the wind by itself. At this stage, you will release the winds through sensitive and skilled use of the elbow directly on reflex points in the navel area. Begin by working on the reflex points that affect the organs. Then use the elbow and knuckles to stimulate certain key points that are the exit passages for the winds on limbs, back, and head to chase and release harmful trapped winds.

When we understand the origin of winds and the problems they create in the body, we will be able to restore health by working closely together with the student. In order to restore the proper balance and circulation of energy in the body, throughout this book we will explain the techniques to chase and release the winds trapped in the body.

Cautions

Before giving a session ask the student about the following:
- Surgeries
- Pacemaker
- IUD (contraceptive intrauterine device)
- Pregnancy
- Medications
- Medical doctor's care

Understanding the Winds

The ancient Taoists discovered powerful internal and external energy forces that affect people in positive or negative ways, and they called them "winds." Good wind is an expression of properly circulating energy or *chi*; it is healthy and beneficial. Negative wind is abnormal and pernicious, and known as sick wind. The West only understands the concept of wind as gas that affects the stomach and intestines or causes heartburn, but winds have different origins and they affect the body in different ways.

DIFFERENT KINDS OF WINDS

Winds of Nature

In nature, the wind is a physical expression of atmospheric pressure and temperature. The wind moves from high- to low-pressure areas, and differences in temperature in the air, land, and water also create wind circulation. Circulating winds set energy in motion.

Some of the winds found in nature can have a detrimental influence on people. Hot, dry winds such as the Santa Ana in California are known to cause feelings of irritability, imbalance, agitation, or depression. In Switzerland, when the mountain wind comes down into the cities, people get headaches and suffer from mood swings, and a greater number of car accidents are reported.

Many people are sensitive to variations in barometric pressure, particularly in extreme situations, such as when the atmospheric pressure is very low just before a heavy thunderstorm or during hurricane and tornado seasons. Common complaints under these circumstances are a sense of heaviness or pressure in the head, a lack of focus, a debilitating sense of lethargy, and immobilizing fatigue.

As to differences in temperature, extreme variations or cold and damp conditions are often seen as the cause of sore throats or head colds that might move down into the lungs. Heat waves also have a marked impact on health, especially for those who are weak or ill.

Winds of Creation

Like many ancient peoples, the Taoists recognized the existence of the sacred energies of the four directions: north, south, east, and west. Archaeological artifacts of many ancient cultures, including those of the Egyptians, the North and South American Indians, and the Siberians, indicate that they all recognized and worked with these energies. In addition to these four major energies, some cultures also recognized a fifth coming from the earth itself. The ancient Taoist sages named these five energies the Winds of Creation.

The Winds of Creation are the central forces in the creation of matter and form and also in the formation of life. They provide the energies that build the bodily organs while we are growing in the womb. Each cosmic wind builds its respective organ system, and the organ systems then build the rest of the body.

After birth, the same winds continue to nourish each of us daily. The most accomplished Taoist masters have cultivated and realized the ability to take their nourishment directly from the sustenance of the sacred winds coursing throughout Earth's atmosphere. The theory behind this ability to function "on breath alone" entails harnessing the winds that create every natural thing on Earth, including the plants and foodstuffs, feeding directly from the primal source that creates the food itself.

The vital organs of the body are "wired" to the earth, galaxy, and universe through the system of the relationship of the five phases of energy, often called the five elements or five grand forces. Please refer to the first Chi Nei Tsang book for a detailed discussion of these micro/macro correspondences.*

Chi Elementals

Another kind of wind energy consists of energized chi, or chi elementals. These exist outside the body but can seriously affect the body's systems. Every thought a person has creates a concentration of such energized chi. This energy resides in the spiritual atmosphere that holds the various kinds of invisible energies that surround us, and anyone can attract it.

If a person is positive and loving, the energy he or she produces is good for everyone. People in need of this energy can soak it up from the atmosphere and use it to feel healthier and to develop themselves spiritually and physically. The greatest healers are able to harvest these elementals constructed of loving chi, not only from their immediate spiritual environment, but from all over the universe. When healers perform miracles, part of the healing power that they pass to the person they are treating may be coming from the love energy that you and millions of other people have generated.

One of the main purposes of the Universal Tao's Cosmic Inner Smile, Cosmic Healing Sounds, and Fusion meditations is to help develop healthier and spiritually advanced individuals capable of transforming emotional energy into refined healthy energy and positive chi elementals. The energy of love, inner joy, kindness, tenderness, gentleness, patience, and balance can set a tone and a positive

---

*Mantak Chia, *Chi Nei Tsang: Chi Massage for the Vital Organs* (Rochester, Vt.: Destiny Books, 2007).

energetic force sufficient to encourage beauty and lead to more human kindness. Individual action can replenish the "tidal pool" of positive energy available to everyone.

Chi elementals originating from negative emotional energy are also stored in the spiritual atmosphere, and these energies can injure people and disrupt the harmony in a community. Just like positive chi elementals, negative chi elementals may be attracted by anyone. These negative energies cannot harm you if your own positive emotional energy is high; but when you are full of fear, anger, sadness, or other negative emotions, it is easier to draw the negative energies that abound in Earth's atmosphere. *Like attracts like.* These elementals can harm your internal organs and upset your emotional balance.

Those who perform black magic and who try to harm others to suit their own personal agendas have learned how to harvest these negative energies from their immediate environment or from other sources throughout the universe. They use the energy to power their negative schemes.

In most ancient cultures, all or at least some members of the group were able to work in the various energy planes and inner worlds of the earth, and they could collect and transform free-floating negative chi elementals before they could do harm. These people were full of vibrant positive energy and had the skill to access other realities and spiritual planes. They would lay their bodies down at night to sleep, and in their spirit bodies they would track down negative energies and transform or ground them before anyone could attract them. They contributed immeasurably to the harmony of their communities.

Internally Generated Winds

The organs in a healthy, well-balanced body have differences in temperature and levels of moisture. These differences serve to maintain homeostasis and create a healthy circulation of energy in the body. However, when elements in the system are not functioning properly, the whole body is thrown out of balance.

The wrong food, poor posture, injuries, negative emotions, and stress block the energy channels in the body, causing problems and generating sick internal winds. What should be free-flowing energy gets stuck and stagnates, affecting all the bodily functions. This stagnation often manifests as headaches, migraines, pain, heartburn, and so forth.

Winds Generated by Food

For the body to function properly, it is very important to provide it with the right kind of fuel. Many foods and certain food combinations are difficult to digest and present a lot of hard work for the body. The Taoist understanding is that when the body has trouble digesting food, wind accumulates in the abdominal cavity and becomes stagnant and sick. In the West, this is known as gas. Since there are many vital organs contained in the abdominal area, wind congestion disrupts the body's natural functions, causing pain and heartburn.

Some of the factors that promote the creation of sick internal winds are inadequate food combinations, eating too many cold or acid-producing foods, eating too quickly, not chewing food properly, and a sedentary lifestyle. The sheer numbers of people who experience the negative impact of sick wind in daily life can be seen in the statistics that show that the best-selling over-the-counter medicines are antigas preparations and antacids.

Most people are very careless about what and how they eat. By becoming aware of your eating habits, you can help your body function better to remain healthy or to heal yourself. The following are a few guidelines that will help you keep a healthy, balanced diet.

Eating Habits: Taking the time to chew food properly is very important. As we chew, the food is mixed with saliva, promoting predigestion. Furthermore, when we eat slowly we give ourselves the opportunity to enjoy the food, and the stomach has time to send the message to the brain when we have eaten enough. The stomach should remain one-quarter to one-third empty, to allow space for digestion to take place.

If it is too full, it will not function properly. For optimal health, it is also important not to eat too late in the evening.

The body needs herbs or other tasty flavors to make it happy. Satisfaction of the senses is important, as tasteless food leaves both mind and body unsettled. Warm, balanced meals that are varied and prepared so as to taste good are satisfying and healthy. A diet of 70 percent carbohydrates; 15 percent high-quality fats such as the essential fatty acids from deep-sea, cold-water fish, organic cold-pressed olive oil, flax seed oil, or borage oil; and 15 percent high-quality, low-fat proteins, helps to encourage the body to work properly.

Drinking at least two to four glasses of water in the morning is very important. Since the stomach is empty in the morning, drinking water at that time can help clean the system of uric acid and create movement in the large intestines. Drinking enough water during the day helps the body to eliminate toxins, lubricate the organs, and keep an appropriate body temperature. However, drinking too much water, wine, or beer with your meal dilutes the digestive enzymes that promote efficient digestion. It is ideal to drink a small glass of liquid during your meal, making sure that it is not too hot or too cold.

Walking after eating facilitates the movement of the digestive system. Massaging your abdominal area and making the spleen sound (see appendix 2) also promotes the production of digestive enzymes and increases the healthy circulation of the winds for digestion.

Eating Appropriate Food: The tissues of the body are very sensitive to accumulations of toxic chemical pesticides and fertilizers. In the United States, two hundred million tons of pesticides are used on domestic crops each year. As pests become resistant, chemical companies introduce new chemicals that are increasingly more powerful and harmful forces.

It is ideal to eat high-quality, organic food grown without artificial pesticides or fertilizers. You may have to pay more, but you get better-tasting, more nutritious food without the toxic load. Furthermore, certified organic food growers tend to be more conscious and to put more love into the food they grow. Their good intentions pay off in the quality and energy that you can actually feel when eating foods grown with care. In order to get all the energy and nutrients from fruits and vegetables, they should be eaten shortly after they are picked. If you do not have access to organic food, it is wise to soak the fruits and vegetables you eat in hydrogen peroxide or aerobic 7 to remove chemical residues and microbes before eating.

If you eat meat, "free-range" meats are best, as they have not been injected with hormones or antibiotics. Also, it is ideal to eat meat within a few hours of the animal being killed. This is often difficult, especially in big cities where meat can sit for three days before it is inspected and sometimes up to two weeks before it is shipped.

Some foods are particularly good for the immune system; these include garlic and onion. They also help detoxify the body, as do vitamin A and beta-carotene (found in most fruits and vegetables). Whenever possible, you should consume vitamins in a sufficient amount directly from a balanced diet. However, if supplements are necessary, be careful not to stress the liver by taking excessive fat-soluble vitamins. Overuse of calcium supplements can leach calcium from the bones.

Sugar, chocolate, and overly refined foods cause the body to heat up and then cool down too fast and the blood vessels to constrict, straining blood circulation and causing pain, stiffness, and soreness. Sugar also inhibits the immune system for four to five hours. These foods should only be eaten occasionally.

Fermentation: The breakdown of food naturally produces gas through the fermentation process. However, excessive fermentation from food that is difficult to digest and poor food combinations (e.g., eating fruit in combination with vegetables, grains, starches, or meats) creates an exaggerated accumulation of gas in the stomach and the digestive tract. Due to the excess gas, the large and small intestines become inflated, causing a sense of indigestion, pressure, and stiffness in the abdomen, which is often tender to the touch. Chemical medicines can also cause indigestion and bloating. Eating steamed pears or apples is a natural way to eliminate gas.

Poor intestinal function causes food and energy stagnation and accumulation of gas. A person with constipation often feels heavy, restless, and ill at ease. A diet that is rich in fiber helps to keep the intestines functioning properly. Good quality fresh vegetables, and ripe seasonal fruits eaten by themselves, can greatly improve bowel function and health. Ripe papaya (rich in papain, a useful digestive enzyme) can also assist in the digestive process.

Acidity and Alkalinity: It is of particular importance to maintain the pH balance of the body. The kidneys filter acid from the blood, helped by the liver, the intestines, and the skin, which serves as a vehicle for acid elimination through perspiration. Extreme acidity disturbs the whole digestive system, as the kidneys are overloaded and excessive mucus forms in the digestive tract. This in turn causes congestion and creates an ideal environment for bacteria and viruses. The joints, cartilage, and connective tissues are also affected as acid deposits in them.

Stress makes the blood acidic, as does eating too many acid-producing foods. You can help your body maintain proper balance by eating the appropriate foods. A diet consisting of 70 to 80 percent alkaline-forming foods is ideal.

The following foods make the blood acid: acid fruits such as cranberries, strawberries, pineapple; bread and most grains (barley, wheat, oats, rye); nuts (except for almonds) and nut oils; seeds (sesame, pumpkin, sunflower); mushrooms; all kinds of meat, eggs, and dairy products (cheese, milk, yogurt, butter, and cream); carbonated drinks, chocolate, coffee, and tea; and all kinds of sugar and syrups.

These foods make the blood alkaline: Most fruits, including the citrus fruits (although they are acid, their effect on the body is to make it more alkaline); millet, buckwheat, sprouted grains, and sprouted seeds; soybeans and lima beans; nonfat milk; honey; oils (olive, soy, sesame, sunflower); legumes and most green vegetables.

Winds Generated by Emotions

Emotions are an important part of the human experience. The Taoist point of view recognizes emotional energy as an indicator of organ health and as a source of valuable guidance toward personal well-being.

Emotions have direct repercussions on the body. Unbridled anger creates a hot, expansive, flashing wind in the body, and fear generates a cold, contracting, internal wind. Jealousy and frustration produce a sour wind.

Emotional changes cause chemical changes. Scientific research, including recent research conducted at UCLA, shows that when people are emotionally upset, certain hormones are released into the body. Researchers suspect that these hormones are produced in the liver and the kidneys, which are known to release hormones into the muscles. (For example, when an animal dies in fear, adrenal hormones are found in the muscles.) Movies normally create in the audience an experience of a wide range of emotions such as fear, happiness, anger, love, and so forth. This is essentially a hormonal ride.

Often, we learn to protect ourselves from feelings that are unpleasant or too intense by ignoring or blocking them, especially through restricting our breath, thereby unconsciously storing these emotions in the body. If these forces go unrecognized and untended, and if they are allowed to stay lodged in the body, they cause imbalance, discomfort, dysfunction, and even serious pain and debilitating illness. The less you feel, the less you possess. Emotional energy that is stuck in the body contributes to ulcers, heart attacks, chest pain, asthma, and many other ailments. There is accumulating proof that repressed emotions are the cause of a great deal of sickness.

The body manifests stuck emotions by expressing symptoms, and these symptoms can guide us into digesting and processing all this trapped emotional energy, which then becomes free-flowing energy that is more and more available to us as we move from ignorance to understanding. But analysis and understanding alone are not enough to release the emotions. Chi Nei Tsang releases them by working on the viscera, the internal and external organ structures, the winds, and the breath. As we breathe into the organs, we release the winds and emotions that are trapped inside.

Generally, we are conditioned by society to suppress our emotions; but when we are provoked or when the load gets to be too much and we can no longer hold our control over these repressed emotions, we explode and dump them on others. This kind of emotional garbage dumping is rampant in our society. Through awareness and the development of simple daily self-care skills, the energy of emotions can be consciously recycled to generate abundant useful positive energy. The Universal Tao's Six Healing Sounds, Inner Smile, and Fusion meditations are great tools to achieve this.

SICK WINDS AFFECT THE ORGANS IN THE BODY

Every organ in the body has an intrinsic wind that flows and circulates in a healthy manner to support the maintenance of vitality. If a person's energies are balanced, he or she rarely has wind problems. However, if there are blockages in the internal energy routes, the winds become renegade forces that throw the body further out of balance.

External attacks of hot, cold, chill, or sick winds that affect human health can be caused by environmental factors such as extremes in the weather, changes of season, toxic substances in the environment, and so forth. Sick winds can penetrate into an imbalanced body through the navel, the back of the head, the forearms, and the lower legs; or they can arise in the interior of the body. The sick winds become trapped in the body, further inhibiting the energy flow. If this congestion is not properly restored to a vital state, it causes degeneration and damage to organs, nerves, and the circulatory, lymphatic, and immune systems, as well as compromising emotional stability.

All the external kinds of winds have a direct effect on the body. Thousands of years ago, the Yellow Emperor, traditional founder of

Chinese medicine, wrote about the harmful effects that the seasonal, macrocosmic winds can have on a body that is ill prepared to receive them. He wrote,

> The east wind arises in spring; its sickness is located in the liver and there are disturbances in the throat and neck. The south wind arises in summer; its sickness is located in the heart and there are disturbances in the chest and ribs. The west wind arises in fall, its sickness is located in the lungs and disturbances arise at the shoulders and the back. The north wind arises in winter; its sickness is located in the kidneys and disturbances arise in the loins and thighs. In the center there is the earth; its sickness is located in the spleen and disturbances arise in the spine.*

The intense blast of the seasonal winds change every three months. But the state of the body's internal microcosmic winds changes every two hours. The internal winds wax and wane several times in a twenty-four-hour recurring cycle. The healing results of acupuncture are dependent on being able to adjust these microcosmic, internal winds. Before acupuncturists apply the needles, they must know the energy state of the client's winds. If the winds are too cold or too hot, too strong or too weak, acupuncturists use their needles to readjust and balance the errant wind. They can drain overabundant wind from the body, or in the case of wind deficiency, they can use their needles as beacons to attract one of the needed microcosmic winds.

From a Taoist perspective, wind attacks can cause arthritis, heart attacks, asthma, migraines, strokes, paralysis, and nerve damage, as well as chronic sharp, stabbing, and unpredictable moving pain. If not treated and abated, the extreme wind conditions underlying these illnesses and complaints can cause serious or permanent damage.

---

*Veith, Ilza, *The Yellow Emperor's Classic of Internal Medicine* (Berkeley: University of California Press, 1949), 110.

USING CHI NEI TSANG TO HEAL
PROBLEMS CREATED BY WINDS

As we said before, when winds are trapped in the body they become evil or sick, preventing energy from circulating freely through the main channels and meridians. This manifests as tangles, blockages, and sick organs. A Chi Nei Tsang practitioner must know how to chase sick winds out of the body before they cause problems. Wind movement is a natural science that you can learn to master.

Just as everyone feels uncomfortable on a day with no wind outside, such is the sense of stagnation in a body riddled with sick wind. The damp, stagnant, smelly conditions found in a wet, musty basement cause the proliferation of molds and bacteria that provoke allergic and respiratory complaints, compromise the immune system, and can result in depression and illness. Clearing such conditions logically involves opening the doors to create the necessary airflow to clear and dry the space out. Likewise, the trapped energy needs to be released from the body so the life force can flow freely inside the person. Since sick winds are composed of chi, when they are expelled from the body they again revert to healthy chi.

Developing skill as a Chi Nei Tsang practitioner requires you to know how to work with winds in order to release them. Normally, massage gives temporary relief to the problems created by wind; but winds run away and hide in different places only to return as soon as the area is left unattended. Sometimes the person actually feels how the pain moves from one place to another. In order to provide lasting relief, you must free the winds.

As the wind exits, the symptoms or manifestations of its presence will disappear. Winds carry toxicity out of the body; they exit as flatulence, burps, yawns, or pops in joints. Skin rashes (e.g., in the crease of the elbows, around the neck, and on the back of the knees) are signs of winds exiting the body, but having a difficult time coming out. In this case, you need to do more detoxification work.

Emotions are an important part of wind elimination. The only way to release emotions is to give yourself permission to feel and possess them, and then release them in a healthy manner. Chi Nei Tsang works simultaneously with the body, the energetic field, and the psyche. The work on the body prevents the mind from hiding and masking the curbed emotions. Increasing awareness and allowing yourself to experience anything that comes up allows you to get back in touch with yourself.

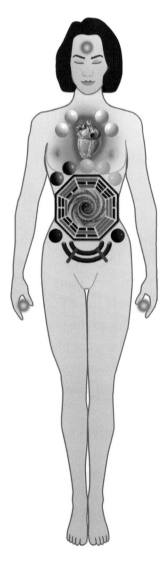

Fig. 1.1. Using Advanced Chi Nei Tsang

Preparation for a Chi Nei Tsang Session

SELF-CARE FOR THE PRACTITIONER

The Universal Tao puts much emphasis on self-care as an essential part of the practice of Chi Nei Tsang. In many modalities, practitioners wear themselves out and get sick themselves.

When you do healing work, there is a chance of picking up sick energy from the person you are working with. The bones are crystal-line in structure so it is easy for energy to get stuck in them. Bone breathing and bone packing, taught in Bone Marrow Nei Kung, help you to keep a high level of energy in your bones and to keep students' sick energy from penetrating beyond your skin. Elixir Chi Kung exercises, and particularly the techniques for swallowing air and saliva, are also important to keep yourself strong and healthy. It is good to train yourself so that even if you do take sick energy from your student, you can immediately send it out from your bones and organs into the ground. It is important for you, as a practitioner, not to allow the sick energy from your student to penetrate into your body and lodge inside one of your organs.

The first Chi Nei Tsang book contains a detailed section on training, protection, and self-care for the practitioner. It covers the

Healing Hands Meditation and the Microcosmic Orbit, Inner Smile, Six Healing Sounds, and Fusion practices, which you use to prevent depletion of energy and to gain the ability to give, take, and transform energy. There are many Universal Tao practices that can be a great complement to your practice of Chi Nei Tsang. For instance, practicing Iron Shirt Chi Kung and Tai Chi Chi Kung can help you to relax and work with your whole body as a unit in a harmonious way. Cosmic Healing is also an effective deterrent to absorbing negative chi, because it focuses on using external energies for healing, rather than your own energy.

PREPARING THE STUDENT FOR THE SESSION

Before you work with a person, hold an interview with him in order to review the level of care that is required for a successful outcome. It is important that students take responsibility for helping themselves, so they need to prepare their bodies before you start working with them and then continue the self-care throughout the treatment.

If people are not willing to take care of themselves, all the effort and energy expense is on your part, and you will be pouring it into a bottomless pit. When this is the case, you need to be very open, gentle, and honest and tell them you cannot work with them unless they are willing to work on themselves too.

Before the session, it is important for your students to detoxify and clean the colon. You can give or send them a printed sheet explaining the procedure. Students should also become aware of their breathing patterns and focus on breathing properly. The following is an overview of what students need to do before the session.

Detoxification

When the body is full of toxins it is impossible for the organs to function properly. By releasing toxicity and tension, you make more free-flowing energy available to balance and heal the organs.

In order to prepare their body for the treatment, for two or three days prior to the session students should drink plenty of water and follow a special diet, eating only the following:

- Brown rice (to carry out poisons from the blood)
- Congee (thin rice soup) made with six parts filtered water to one part organic rice
- Vegetable soup (may be seasoned with a bit of organic chicken, but the chicken should not be eaten)
- Juice from green vegetables and leaves (i.e., spinach), which are naturally rich in chlorophyll
- Fresh, natural fruit and vegetable juice

Cleaning the Colon

When the colon is clogged, the body becomes more acid and reabsorbs toxins that it intended to eliminate. After one day of stagnation, the large intestines send the toxins back for storage, causing discomfort and pain.

For Chi Nei Tsang treatment to be successful, the colon must be clean, otherwise you simply massage old stool in the large and small intestines. Some people can carry many pounds of impacted fecal matter and much unfriendly bacteria in the colon. A great deal of sick energy can accumulate in old, putrefied stool. My teacher would never do Chi Nei Tsang on someone whose colon was not clean.

Colonics can be very helpful in moving out old mucus, gas, and hard impacted fecal matter, and they also help restore proper peristaltic action of the intestines. Parasites can be eliminated with colonic irrigation and the use of fresh raw organic garlic cloves ground and filtered into the water. (Cooking garlic even slightly eliminates its detoxifying and antiparasitic properties.)

To support the colonic cleansing, it is good to massage the sigmoid colon in the lower left quadrant, then the descending colon, the two upper flexures in the corners under the spleen and liver, the transverse colon, and finally the ascending colon and ileocecal valve. For a more detailed explanation, refer to the first-level Chi Nei Tsang book, Mantak Chia, *Chi Nei Tsang* (Rochester, Vt.: Destiny Books, 2007).

To release and facilitate the movement of waste through the intestines while doing a colonic treatment it is good to take a teaspoon of psyllium seed husks and a tablespoon of bentonite mixed in an 8-ounce glass of room-temperature water, and then drink another glass of water.

It is good to cleanse the colon two or three times per year and after periods of travel or dietary excess. There are many well-trained, competent colon therapists, and in addition, home colonic units with slant boards are now available. At Tao Garden, our training center in Chiang Mai, Thailand, where there is plenty of fresh air, filtered water, and sunshine, we offer a special seven-day cleansing program.

The Importance of Breathing Properly

The way we breathe is the way we feel. It reflects on the way we stand and move and how we perceive ourselves in the world. Most people have a habit of not breathing deeply, not fully inhaling and exhaling, especially during periods of stress.

By blocking our breath, we block our access to feelings. We protect ourselves from experiencing certain feelings, and these become trapped energy in the organs, generating imbalances and wind problems. Getting sick is the way our body draws our attention to the blocked and neglected organs. As we breathe into them, we release the winds and emotions that are trapped inside.

Breathing appropriately means using the diaphragm. Relax the chest and breathe in deeply, drawing the air into the abdomen, feeling it expand in all directions (front, back, and sides). Expel the breath by drawing the abdomen up, squeezing in on all sides of the abdomen, and breathing out through the nose (fig. 2.1). In cases of hernia, asthma, heart attack, and strokes, proper breathing allows the wind to move out.

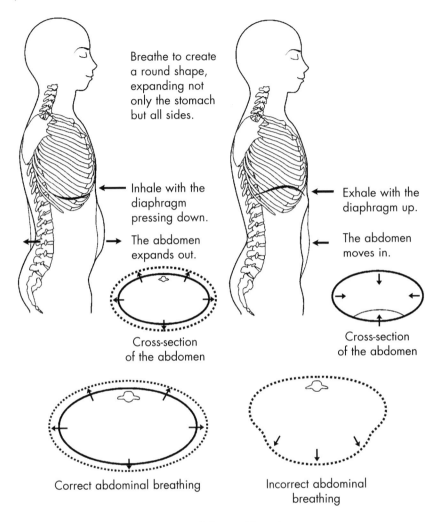

Breathe to create a round shape, expanding not only the stomach but all sides.

Inhale with the diaphragm pressing down.

The abdomen expands out.

Cross-section of the abdomen

Exhale with the diaphragm up.

The abdomen moves in.

Cross-section of the abdomen

Correct abdominal breathing

Incorrect abdominal breathing

Fig. 2.1. Abdominal breathing

The Tao Yin exercises from the Universal Tao series are very helpful to teach students to breathe deeply into the lower abdomen and progressively feel the breath expand upward, filling the entire lungs as the diaphragm moves down. For more information on the Tao Yin exercises, see Mantak Chia, *Energy Balance through the Tao* (Rochester, Vt.: Destiny Books, 2005).

Deep Belly Laughing

Deep belly laughing is the best form of breath work. Laughing from the abdomen four or five times per day stimulates the intestines to move waste out and promotes the circulation of blood and lymph, eliminating energy stagnation (fig. 2.2). Also, as you move from the sympathetic to the parasympathetic system with laughter, the blood becomes more alkaline.

Laughter stimulates a healing set of brain chemicals and fosters self-loving, joyous feelings. Dr. Bernie Siegel's work on self-healing through laughter shows that people have healed themselves from serious illnesses with laugh therapy.

Fig. 2.2. Laughing practice

Basic Chi Nei Tsang Techniques

WORKING WITH THE STUDENT: FOUNDATIONS FOR ALL THE WORK

As you work with a student, it is important to establish an atmosphere of trust and openness. If you are insensitive with your words or your movements (for instance, if you move too quickly or with too much force), the student will be unable to relax and release the stored emotions and blockages. If a student senses that you can be trusted and that you are there to assist in her learning, it will be easier for her to feel safe and open up to you. Be sure to be patient all through the process. Be sensitive, and respect the student's feelings and space.

This work requires a deep connection with yourself and with your student in order to maintain a sense of where the student is and what she is going through. The following are a few points that are necessary to achieve a good connection:

- Always stay in your center and accompany your student through her process from that place. At all times be aware of your good intentions, and work with respect and love.
- Feel yourself firmly rooted to the earth, and connect to the

energy from the earth and the heaven instead of using your own energy, which would soon be depleted.

- The more relaxed you are, the more you will be able to be deeply in touch with your student. Your student will easily perceive any tension, nervousness, or haste on your side.

- Synchronize your breathing with your student's. In this way, you will be aware of any changes (e.g., gasping, shallow breathing, or sudden intakes of breath). These changes in breathing patterns may be due to excessive or too sudden pressure from you as you work on her body, or fear or reluctance from the student to your touching something that is stored in the particular area where you are working. By being connected with the person, you can encourage her to keep on breathing deeply, allowing her to touch and release emotional blockages and tension.

- Elicit feedback from your student, and be sensitive with her perceptions and sensations. Anything that she tells you is a source of information that is an important piece in the overall puzzle.

- Always observe the face of the person you are working with. Sometimes a student may not be able to express what is going on verbally. Information is also transmitted by facial expressions.

- There is a good chance that students will touch deep emotional wounds that they had not been able to contact or release before. As the practitioner, you are responsible for being there for them. Honor their process and support them. Sometimes your student's reactions may trigger a feeling or a response in you. Acknowledge it to yourself and then let it go; or put it aside so you can deal with it after the session. Be careful not to vent it on your student.

- Some of the points treated with Chi Nei Tsang are very delicate and private. Take care to ask permission from the student and work very respectfully and comfortably with these points. The student will sense if there is any nervousness or hesitation on your part.

Cautions

Students with pacemakers should consult with their heart specialists before you treat them with Chi Nei Tsang. The Inner Smile, the Six Healing Sounds, and the Microcosmic Orbit are great for reducing stress and are always recommended.

If a woman is wearing an intrauterine device (IUD) to prevent conception, be careful to avoid massaging the area of the uterus. If a woman is pregnant you should also avoid the uterus, but massaging the abdomen and the intestines will help create an appropriate space for the baby. Sometimes when babies kick it is because they are uncomfortable and feel crowded when their mother's abdomen is bloated or full of gas. Special techniques for working on pregnant women will appear in a forthcoming book.

Chi, the Mind, and the Body

Remember—and remind your student—

Where the mind goes, the chi goes; where the chi goes, the blood goes; where the blood goes, the lymph goes; where the lymph goes, the muscles go; where the muscles go, the tendons go; where the tendons go, the bones go.

This also applies to the movement of the winds, and with conscious intention and practice, we are able to move the winds.

Student's Position

It is much easier to move the winds if your student is lying on his back with his legs straight. The knees may be supported with a low pillow. When working on your student's back, if you are not using a massage table with a cut-out for the face to rest in, you may put shiatsu rolls or soft, shapeable pillows under the armpits and a soft pillow under the forehead (fig. 3.1). Make sure not to stress your student's neck.

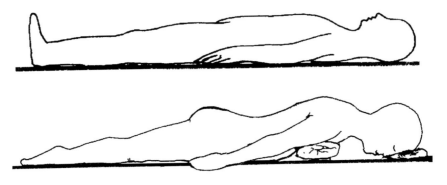

Fig. 3.1. Student's position

LOOKING FOR PATTERNS

Scan your student's abdomen closely using the back of your hand to sense temperature and the palm for sensing changes in pressure and energy level. Relax, sense, and trust your instincts. This is not a mental exercise. Develop sensitivity and skill in cultivating, sending, and receiving healthy chi.

Observe the shape of the navel and look for patterns of movement in the navel and the rib cage. Feel where there are depressions, holes, protrusions, bumps, heat, or cold. Sense your student's body as a landscape and visualize the wind currents. There are no coincidences in Chi Nei Tsang. The patterns you observe are not random; they signify places where stagnation, excess, or build-up of wind are calling for attention. Observing all of these aspects will allow you to develop a strategy that you can continuously evaluate and modify as you work.

THE MERIDIAN SYSTEM

By becoming familiar with the energy meridians of the body and by learning to use the healing energy in your work with the acupuncture points and special Chi Nei Tsang treatment points covered in this book, you can greatly assist your students in their self-healing process. We have provided drawings of the key points for the meridians throughout the book. Appendix 1 contains plates with all the Chi Nei Tsang points, as well as the description of their exact location and their correspondence to traditional acupuncture points. Be aware that some Chi Nei Tsang points are not so precise and can refer to a palm-sized area. Copy the charts for your own use. We also recommend that you enlarge them and hang them on the wall in the space where you practice, with the corresponding descriptions of the points at hand so that you can use them as reference while you are working. They can be very useful in formulating an approach to your work during the diagnostic interview before you begin each session.

The Difference between Acupuncture Points and Chi Nei Tsang

Acupuncture charts of the meridians and points can only serve as a beginning point of reference. The acupuncture points indicated on most charts generally depict superficial points on the meridians that are close enough to the surface of the body to allow access to them by inserting needles on the skin. The charts generally do not show that an entire meridian runs deep into the interior of the body through areas that are much too remote to reach with a needle.

For instance, all the needle points for the heart meridian are on the arms, but the heart meridian begins at a deep level in the tissues of the heart itself. It includes a deep pathway that runs down the centerline, through the diaphragm, ending in the small intestine. It also follows another route that leaves the heart, travels up the esophagus through the tongue and around the mouth, and ends just under the eye.

The wind affects the specific organs and all the areas throughout the entire meridian. The Chi Nei Tsang techniques for removing winds require that you learn to use hand, finger, knuckle, and elbow, and use appropriate pressure at or near key access points on the meridians.

Wind Access Points

The winds collect in certain areas that often correspond to the standard acupuncture points. These points are all contained in the Chi Nei Tsang plates. The winds collect in overflowing "ponds" near the points, so you do not have to hit the point as precisely as an acupuncturist does. You will have more leeway; you may even have to search nearby for the wind access areas. Practical experience and development of chi-sensitive hands will serve you greatly. There is no substitute for proper instruction with certified Universal Tao Chi Nei Tsang teachers, who you can locate through the resources at the back of this book and on the Universal Tao web site.

It is important to feel energy deficiencies or excesses, as well as tangles, twists, swelling, and so forth. You will be drawn to certain areas where there are problems and this is where you can work to restore the proper flow of energy. The most sensitive point is the "right point." As you press the points, you will feel the energy move or drain. When the wind moves, the pain will move.

APPROACHING THE NAVEL

When a baby is still in its mother's womb, it receives oxygen and nourishment through the umbilicus. All the organs and every part of the body are directly connected to it. The navel is a particularly intimate place and the center of an individual's personal universe.

Many emotions are stored in the abdomen, and it is only through relaxation and trust that you will be able to guide your student into letting go of the blocked energies stuck in the area. If you press too quickly or cause too much pain, the student's organs will contract in shock, pain, or fear, and the blockages will get worse. As long as the student can breathe into the pain, it will eventually be released. But if the breath is blocked, the body will contract in another area and the pain will only momentarily move to this new place.

Work on Pressure Points

The practice of Chi Nei Tsang involves pressing points on the body that relate to the organs and that open the wind gates for the winds to come out. Much of the work in Advanced Chi Nei Tsang is done with the elbow on the navel and with attention to some related points on the head and limbs.

Elbow Technique

Entering your student's navel with your elbow requires you to have a sense of your own center and your own breath, and to be sensitive to your student's personal space and breath. The more relaxed you are, the more you will be in contact with your student and sense what is happening in the body. In addition, the less contracted your muscles are, the easier it will be for the chi to flow, allowing you to move the winds. If you work from the left side, use your left elbow, and from the right side, use your right elbow. As you work with your student, keep the following points in mind:

1. Learn to use your body in such a way that you will not get tired. You should be as comfortable as possible. A massage table is very practical when you are working with your elbow. If you use one, make sure the height is appropriate for you before your student gets on it. It should be low enough that you can reach your student's body, but not so low that you must bend your back. Whether you work on the floor or at a table, make sure to keep your back straight, your head pulled up, and your chin tucked in. Bend from

the lower back in order to keep your spine straight (figs. 3.2–3.3). Avoid bending your neck, as this jams the Jade Pillow and closes your throat, creating a cloudy mind. Regular practice of Tai Chi Chi Kung and Iron Shirt Chi Kung can help you keep your spine straight and your throat open, and improve your posture.

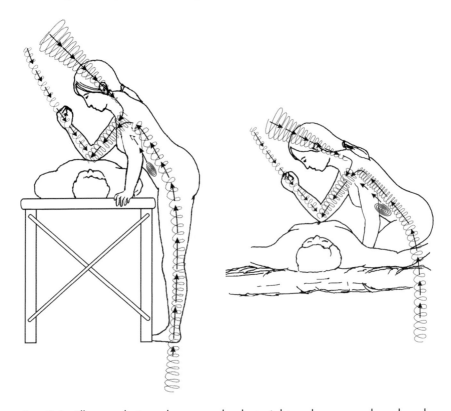

Fig. 3.2. Elbow technique: keep your back straight and your muscles relaxed. Move the body from the lower tan tien as one unit.

2. Keep your upper arms, shoulders, and neck relaxed. Relaxed muscles will facilitate the flow of chi.
3. Move from your lower tan tien so your elbow will move as one unit with the body.
4. To apply pressure on the points, use your body weight and not the muscles of your arms and back.

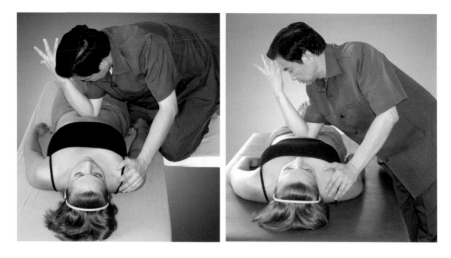

Fig. 3.3. Elbow technique

O Elbow Position

The elbow is a powerful tool, and you need to be careful to apply the right amount of pressure. When you bend your elbow 45 degrees, the pressure will be stronger than when you bend it 90 degrees (fig. 3.4).

45°

The pressure is more intense at 45°.

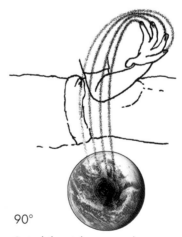

90°

Spiral the sick energy down into the earth.

Fig. 3.4. Pressing with the elbow

○ Locating the Points

When you are dealing with a specific wind, the procedure will describe which points to work on. To locate the exact points where you will use your elbow, you need to sense the area with your fingers and palm first. Once you have more experience, you will be able to locate other points that need work. By spiraling your hand above your student's navel, you will be able to identify the stuck winds that obstruct the whole flow of energy. You will also be able to alter the order in which to work on the points or create your own sequences.

○ Pressing the Points

1. Once you have located the point where you will work, put your elbow on it. As your student exhales, press by slowly and gently leaning your weight into it until you feel resistance from the wind. By moving gently and carefully from your lower tan tien, you will be able to sense how deep to go.

2. When you push into the navel, take care to support your weight with your other hand on the table. Always observe your student's face, and communicate with her. If you push in too quickly or with too much force, it is possible to cause the sympathetic nervous system to respond by tightening. This work takes more energy than merely working with your muscles. Muscles will not move wind. Once you are in deep contact, stop moving and hold the elbow still. You will be able to feel the wind struggling.

3. Sense your student's navel beginning to loosen and relax. Use your elbow to spiral on the point, the movement coming from your entire torso. As you release the tangles and knots, you will feel the winds gathering and the energy moving. As the sick wind moves, the pain will move. When you move the winds out, the chi will move and fill the space that was previously occupied by sick wind. Continue to watch your student's face and be aware of her breathing as a source of direct feedback on what she is experiencing.

4. As your student inhales into the abdomen, let your elbow rise up slightly, but do not lose contact. If you know the Tai Chi exercise called Sticky Hands, its principle—"Never let loose, never hold too tight"—will help you to develop your elbow technique. Ask the student to continue breathing "around" your elbow. Guide the student to exhale any cloudy, gray, sick, or dense energy out through your elbow and through her fingers and toes into the earth.

5. When you're working on the navel points, you can touch a related point. For example, while working on the navel points for the sixth wind, the left hand can hold points 13 and/or 15 on the face.

○ Allowing the Wind to Leave through Palm and Fingers

If you remain relaxed and centered, eventually you will feel the wind move through your palm and the tips of your fingers. Your palm should be open and slightly cupped and your fingers open and pointed upward. Keeping your hand relaxed will help to coax and guide the winds. Keep your hand away from your face so the sick wind can come out through your palm (see fig. 3.4 on page 31). You will sense the winds moving, and the area may feel like a deflating balloon.

○ Removing Your Elbow

Ask your student to inhale deeply, pushing your elbow out. Move to the next point and repeat the procedure.

◎ *Finger and Knuckle Work*

Some points are too delicate for the elbow or they require more precision. For these, use the fleshy part of the finger or thumb.

If your fingertip is not enough to apply the necessary force, use the second knuckle of the index finger or the second knuckles of the index, middle, and ring fingers; use the middle knuckle to press the exact point, and use the other knuckles as support to work on a wider area and to make the work less pointed in sensitive areas (fig. 3.5).

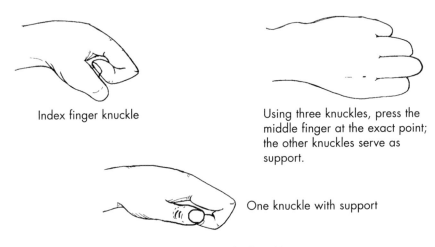

Index finger knuckle

Using three knuckles, press the middle finger at the exact point; the other knuckles serve as support.

One knuckle with support

Fig. 3.5. Using the knuckle

When you work with your knuckles and fingers, make sure you keep your arm straight so that the pressure comes from your whole body and not from the muscles in the arm.

Chasing the Winds

When winds are trapped in the body, they are compressed, and if they are given an opportunity to move out into a bigger, open space where they can be free, they will. The body has to find a strategy to cope with stressful situations, tensions, and internal conflicts. Winds are the results of such situations and have no choice but to follow the body's pattern of internal tensions. Intention goes a long way in gathering the winds and sending them out. Working with the elbow to chase the winds is a longer procedure than just opening the wind gates and chasing the winds described in *Chi Nei Tsang*, the first-level Chi Nei Tsang book. Using your intention, willpower, and inner voice can involve talking to the winds, encouraging them to gather and move out of the body.

◎ *Creating Space for the Winds to Gather*

Releasing the tension around the navel creates a space where the sick winds can gather in the way that water pools when you make a hole in the earth. It is an invitation for the winds to come to this area. Your work is to collect them there and then assist them by creating movement so they can leave the body, making space for healthy chi.

◎ *Moving the Winds*

The work with the elbow or fingers on the different points is meant to call and direct the winds. Rather than chasing them throughout the whole body, be observant and feel, sensing them as they move. It is much like the intuitive feeling of cooking. Once you start to read the body, there is no place for the winds to hide. They will move as you untie knots and release the tension in your student's body.

When the winds move, they will sometimes go up to your student's face or into other areas of the body where he is used to storing pain, such as the back, the hips, or the shoulders. As the winds move from the area, the pain will go away.

◎ *Allowing the Winds to Exit*

After a while you may feel the wind begin to move out of the student's navel and other areas of the body. Sometimes the cool energy will feel like a breeze, and while you work with your elbow, you will feel it on your forearm. This cool air can make the hairs on your arm stand up and cause goosebumps. Often the sick wind feels icy. Astute observers standing near you can often feel the temperature difference in the cloud of cool air enveloping your presence and sometimes the whole room. This phenomenon always turns those who are skeptical about the existence of internal winds into believers.

As the sick wind moves out and a healthy circulation of chi is restored, the student will experience a sense of relief and well-being.

Some students may feel differences in temperature or sense colors, and often they will feel the need to belch. This is a good sign that the winds are moving out.

1. Wait for all the wind to exit until you do not feel it anymore, and then slowly withdraw your elbow by allowing the student to push it out with his inhalation.

2. In order to clear all the winds from the body, we must open all the doors to let them out. Therefore, it is also important to work on the related points, on feet, arms, and head. Otherwise, we might push the winds out through the channels but then block the final exit point, creating congestion, like a closed door in a theater when everyone is trying to leave. The winds above the diaphragm will exit through the hands, and the winds below it will exit through the feet.

3. To help the winds move out, prompt your student to wiggle toes and fingers and exhale any cloudy, gray, or sick energy out through them. Teach students that they can use their intention to send the winds out. The Six Healing Sounds can also be of assistance. While it may take several sessions of encouragement and guidance, most students will gain their own unique sense of how it feels as the winds move, and they will develop confidence in their own experience of moving them.

Flushing and Venting

After you have worked on your student's body and once all the doors are open and the winds are moving out, encourage all the remaining winds to exit. Explain the process to your student.

1. With your open palm above your student's navel (6–12 inches from the body), spiral counterclockwise 18 to 36 times. This will create a vortex that will gather the remaining winds.

2. With long, sweeping movements, direct the wind down your

student's legs and out through the toes and into the ground. Your hand should travel the entire path that you want the wind to follow. If the wind you are flushing out is above the diaphragm, guide it down the arms, through the fingers, and into the ground (fig. 3.6). The earth can accept the sick and negative energy and transform it into useful energy.

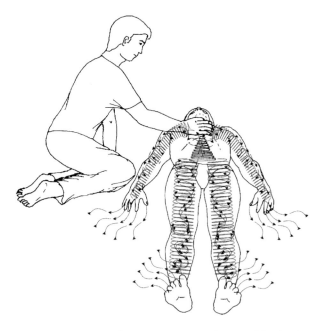

Fig. 3.6. Drawing the remaining winds out of the body

3. If the winds are stubborn, you may use a green or blue light to help carry the winds out and energize the area. Contact the green light of the universe by visualizing lush green forests. Absorb this energy through your throat, and let it activate the green energy in your liver. Contact the blue light from the sky and the deep blue of the ocean, absorb it through your throat, and let it activate the blue energy in the kidneys. A more detailed description of this procedure is explained in our book, *Taoist Cosmic Healing.**

*Mantak Chia, *Taoist Cosmic Healing* (Rochester, Vt.: Destiny Books, 2003).

Working Procedures for Advanced Chi Nei Tsang

The following are the procedures to follow in an advanced Chi Nei Tsang session with a student. Before beginning any Chi Nei Tsang session, you should always ground your student into the earth to access the earth's healing energy (fig. 4.1).

Grounding Your Student

1. First ground yourself down to the core of the earth and down to the galaxy on the other side of the earth.
2. Be aware of your student's navel and the soles of the feet and ground the student down to the earth.
3. Empty your student's energy down to the ground so that the earth's healing energy can be brought up to your student.

BASIC CHI NEI TSANG

In order to work with the winds in your student's body, you must first integrate the procedures of Basic Chi Nei Tsang. This involves carefully

Fig. 4.1. Grounding your student

sensing and touching the abdomen; clearing the large and small intestines; toning, detoxifying, and pumping the organs; and clearing the lymphatic system. (Refer to the first Chi Nei Tsang book, *Chi Nei Tsang: Chi Massage for the Vital Organs*.) If the person's abdomen is full of knots and tangles, the winds will not be able to circulate and leave the body. Releasing the abdomen may take a few sessions. Once you have released the main blockages, you can then begin the work on the winds.

WORKING ON THE WINDS

This work includes releasing the navel area and then chasing and flushing out the winds as described in the following exercise. Chapter 5 of this book provides a detailed explanation of the procedure to follow for specific winds and their manifestation. Most of the work is done with the elbow on the student's navel and by working on related points in the back, head, and limbs.

Opening the Wind Gates

In this practice we'll make "traps" for the winds. One trap is created by using the "elbow in the navel." A second trap comes from "opening the navel with the thumbs." A third and quite powerful trap is "making space in the pakua." These traps present an open space for the winds to move to, and from there you can easily flush them and vent them down the legs and out of the feet.

Elbow in the Navel

In this level of Chi Nei Tsang, one way of opening the wind gates is through the use of the elbow placed directly on the student's navel. In order to explain this procedure, we will figuratively divide the navel area into a 360 degree circle, split up into four sections. It is equivalent to a compass lying on the person's belly. When we talk about the left or right side, we refer to the left or right side on your student's body. The top of the navel is south/180 degrees. The left side is west/270 degrees. Below the navel is north/0/360 degrees. The right side of the navel is east/90 degrees (fig. 4.2). Every degree of the navel circle connects to a different part of the body:

180°–270° describes the upper left quadrant of the abdomen.
270°–360° describes the lower left quadrant.
0°–90° describes the lower right quadrant.
90°–180° describes the upper right quadrant.

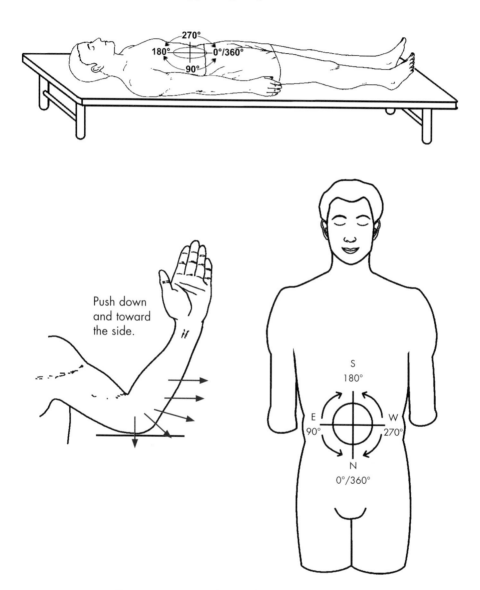

Fig. 4.2. Opening the wind gates with the elbow

The procedure to open the wind gates with the elbow is the following:

1. Place your elbow on the navel and press down.
2. Holding the pressure, move your elbow out toward the left side of your student's body at 270°. Repeat this movement, working from the center outward as you move toward 180° and then from 180° back to 270°. Rest, twist the wrist and fingers, and let the sick winds out of your fingertips down into the earth (fig. 4.3). Release the pressure, go back to the center of the navel, and press down and out from the center to 280°, then from the center to 290°, continuing until you have worked your way to 360° and from 360° back toward 270°. When you are finished with this lower left quadrant, ask your student to breathe deeply into the navel to push your elbow out.
3. Flush the winds down the legs and out through the toes.

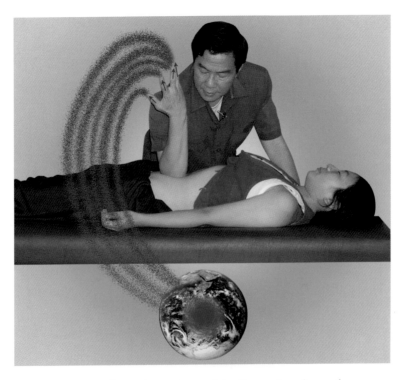

Fig. 4.3. Sick winds spiral out of the fingers into the earth.

4. Repeat this procedure on the lower right quadrant from 90° toward 0° and then from 0° toward 90°. Repeat the procedure once more on the upper right quadrant, working from 90° toward 180°. This will open the whole navel, creating a place for the wind to gather and releasing the tightness of the abdomen. For people who have back pain, this work will greatly reduce the back pain. Flush and vent 15–20 times until you feel the navel is warm.

⊙ Opening the Navel with the Thumbs

Taoists believe that there are trapped winds in the intestines and abdomen and also in all the tendons from the body that join around the navel. Release the navel by pressing your thumbs on the ring muscle of the navel and pushing down and in opposite directions (fig. 4.4) for an approximate count of 15.

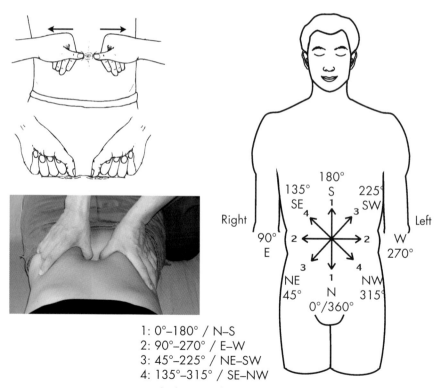

1: 0°–180° / N–S
2: 90°–270° / E–W
3: 45°–225° / NE–SW
4: 135°–315° / SE–NW

Fig. 4.4. Push down and in opposite directions.

Your aim is to stretch the muscle below the skin, so you will need to place your fingers on the sides of the navel and not inside. Be careful not to hurt the skin as you push in opposite directions. Flush and vent 15–20 times.

❂ Making Space in the Pakua

Opening the area around the navel following the shape of a pakua discharges tensions from the body, releases pinched or tight nerves, and reestablishes the proper flow in blood vessels and lymph channels. This follows the Later Heaven pakua energy flow. To know more about the pakuas, see *Cosmic Fusion.** In Fusion I, we learn about the relationships between the organs and the different *kuas* (forces). For example, the kidneys are related to kan (water) in the north and the liver to chen (thunder and lightning) in the east. In Advanced Chi Nei Tsang, we relate the organs not to the kuas but to the reflexology points of the organs themselves. For example, the left kidney is at the Western Gate (4) and the right kidney at the Eastern Gate (3) (see fig. 4.6).

With the side of your hand, the heel of your palm, or the thumbs, press into the abdomen with both hands, one pushing on the other (fig. 4.5). If you feel too much wind when pressing down, stop, flush and vent down and out. This will make a big space and force the winds that are stuck in the organs and body to come and gather in the pakua area.

Press the eight sides of the pakua in the following order (fig. 4.6).

1. Press the Northern Gate (related to the bladder and the sexual organs, on the bottom of the pakua, at 0°/360°).
2. Press the Southern Gate (related to the heart, on the top of the pakua, at 180°).
3. Press the Eastern Gate (related to the right kidney, on your student's right side, at 90°).

---

*Mantak Chia, *Cosmic Fusion* (Rochester, Vt.: Destiny Books, 2007).

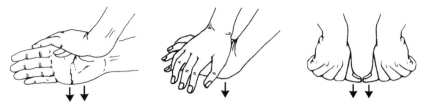

Use the side of the hand or bottom of the palm (wrist), or use the thumbs.

Fig. 4.5. Pressing the side of the pakua

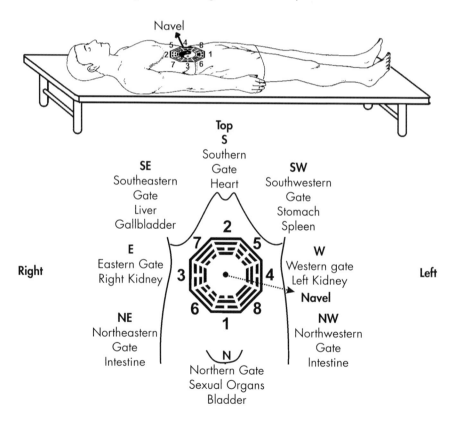

Fig. 4.6. Sequence for releasing the wind gates on the
pakua and organs affected

4. Press the Western Gate (related to the left kidney, on your student's left side, at 270°).

5. Press the Southwestern Gate (related to the stomach and spleen, on your student's upper left, at 225°).

6. Press the Northeastern Gate (related to the intestines, on your student's lower right, at 45°).

7. Press the Southeastern Gate (related to the liver and gallbladder, on your student's upper right, at 135°).

8. Finally, press the Northwestern Gate (related to the intestines, on your student's lower left, at 315°).

9. Flush and vent 15–20 times.

10. Have the student place her fingers on the navel and have her feel a fire inside the lower tan tien burning out the sick winds (fig. 4.7). The fire drives out the cold and damp.

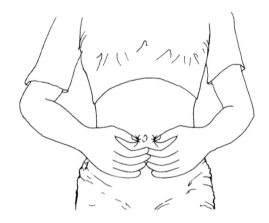

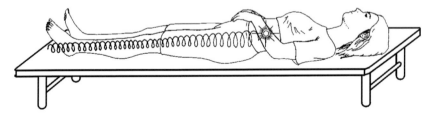

Fig. 4.7. Let the fire burn out the sick winds.

☉ Closing the Session

When you perform Chi Nei Tsang, the blood and energy concentrate in the abdomen. Before your student gets up at the end of the session, guide her to do "monkey dancing." Ask her to lie on her back and to raise her arms and legs toward the ceiling and to shake them enthusiastically and loosely, and to laugh while breathing deeply in the abdomen (fig. 4.8). This will help activate the lymph and blood circulation (fig. 4.9).

Fig. 4.8. Monkey dancing

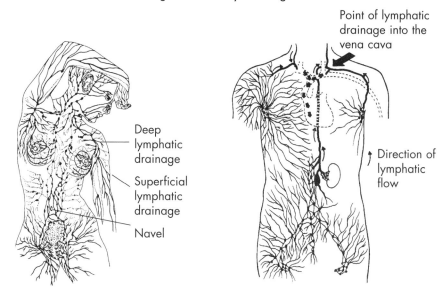

Point of lymphatic
drainage into the
vena cava

Deep
lymphatic
drainage

Superficial
lymphatic
drainage

Navel

Direction of
lymphatic
flow

Fig. 4.9. Lymphatic drainage system

ENCOURAGING STUDENTS TO WORK ON THEMSELVES

It is important to teach your students to do Advanced Chi Nei Tsang on themselves between sessions. At the end of the session, point out to them the areas that were particularly tight or congested; it is important that they continue to work on releasing them at home. Show them how to work on themselves using their fingers with their hands relaxed and elbows extended to their sides. Their shoulders, neck, and arms should be relaxed and connected to the spine.

Tell your students that it is important for them to be responsible for their health and to take the time to work on themselves. If they are confident of their own ability to care for themselves, they will feel more positive, stronger, and freer. Refer them to any additional practices that could help them to deal with their situation. In the Taoist way, suggest that they simplify their lives by allowing one unnecessary thing to fall away each day. This will settle their organs and calm their minds.

A daily routine of moderate exercise (for instance, walking briskly) activates blood circulation and movement of the lymphatic system and keeps the body in good shape. It is also good to massage the belly every day, stimulating the four corners of the intestines: (fig. 4.10) the ileocecal valve (in the lower right abdomen, approximately at the midpoint between the navel and the right pelvic bone); the hepatic flexure in the right upper abdomen (under the bottom right corner of the rib cage and under the liver); the splenic flexure (in the upper left quadrant of the abdomen under the bottom of the left rib cage); and the sigmoid colon (from the lower left corner of the abdomen between the midline of the abdomen and the left pelvic bone). Following a healthy diet is also very important.

In the way of the Tao, each individual in the world is responsible for his own enlightenment and well-being. As Universal Tao Chi Nei Tsang practitioners and teachers, we are responsible for encouraging our students to be themselves and to grow. As they do their work and feel the results, they will want to do more for themselves.

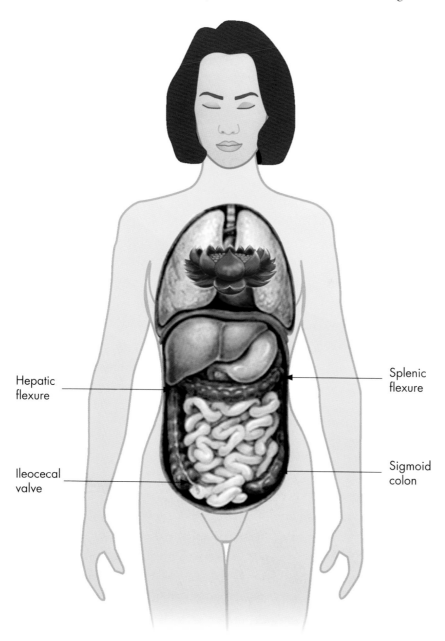

Hepatic
flexure

Splenic
flexure

Ileocecal
valve

Sigmoid
colon

Fig. 4.10. Four corners of the intestines

5

Working on the Winds

When dealing with each of the winds, you must always begin by opening the wind gates, the navel, and the pakua, and releasing the knots and tangles in the navel area (with the procedure described in the first Chi Nei Tsang book). You must do this in order to create a space for the winds to pool and to open the way for them to move and exit the body (see chapter 4).

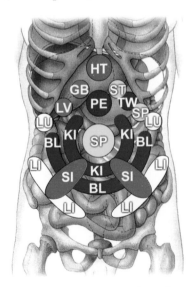

LU	Lung
LV	Liver
GB	Gall Bladder
HT	Heart
ST	Stomach
TW	Triple Warmer
SP	Spleen
PE	Pericardium
KI	Kidneys
BL	Bladder
SI	Small intestine
LI	Large intestine

Fig. 5.1. Chi Nei Tsang chart showing areas where you can access and balance the energy of the organs (based on a drawing in *Zen Shiatsu* by Shiyuto Masunaga)

Working on the Navel

The following describes the procedure you will use to work on the points on the navel defined for each wind. Refer to chapter 3 for the detailed explanation of use of the elbow. When using your elbow, always connect to the first wind with the other hand and guide the wind flow around the circle. The points defined as left and right are based on the left and right side of your student's body. In the last point, chase the wind out.

1. Find the point you will work on with your elbow.
2. Press gently as your student exhales.
3. Release tangles and knots.
4. Spiraling with your elbow, feel the winds starting to gather and the energy starting to move. As the winds move, the area may feel like a deflating balloon.
5. When you feel that the winds have moved from that point, allow your student to push your elbow out as he inhales.
6. Flush the winds out by spiraling with your hand over the area that you have worked on, and then guide them with your hands down your student's legs or arms and out through the toes or fingers. As the winds exit, direct them into the ground. Do this after each point.
7. Move on to the next point.
8. As you work, encourage your student to breathe, exhaling any cloudy gray or sick energy out through the toes and fingers.

The First Wind

Wind That Attacks the Liver, the Pericardium, and the Heart

This wind rises from the small intestines and spleen and attacks the liver, pericardium, and heart, making them weak and tired. Symptoms usually manifest as a burning itching feeling and restless sleep, sometimes accompanied by a burning rash. The liver and heart tend to hold heavy-duty emotions such as anger, envy, and hatred. Working on the first wind can elicit a strong emotional release.

Pressing the Navel Points for the First Wind

Use your elbow to press the navel points for the first wind (fig. 5.2). Follow the arrows in the illustration. This will help spiral all winds out from the organs. Remember to flush out the wind after pressing each point.

1. Press point 35, located just above the navel, on the left side.
2. Press point 35 on the right side.
3. Press point 32, located below the navel toward the outside of the body, on the left side.
4. Press point 32 on the right side.
5. Press point 37, located on a line right above the navel, on the right side.
6. Press point 37 on the left side.
7. Press point 30, located below the lower end of the sternum. Be careful not to press on the tip of the sternum, as it is very delicate.

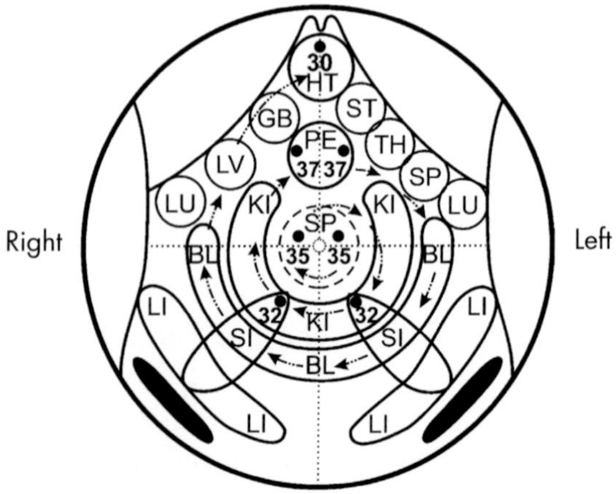

Fig. 5.2. Navel points for the first wind

☯ Releasing Wind from the Liver

To release the wind from the liver, first observe the shape of your student's rib cage. If there is a problem, the ribs may be raised on one side.

1. Loosen the area under the ribs and massage the liver (figs. 5.3 and 5.4). Have the student do the liver sound, "sh-h-h-h-h-h-h." (For a detailed explanation of the Six Healing Sounds procedure, refer to appendix 2 in this book, or to *Chi Nei Tsang*, pages 100–106.)

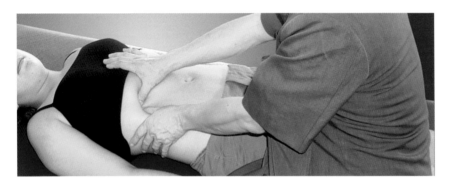

Fig. 5.3. Massage the liver with both thumbs.

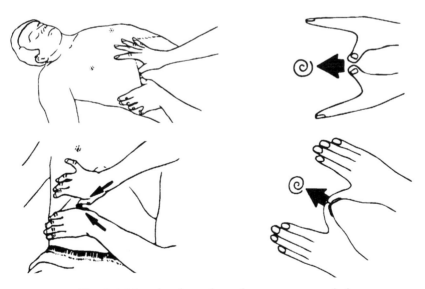

Fig. 5.4. Vary thumb angle and pressure as needed.

2. Press your knuckles on and between the rib bones all around the bottom of the rib cage on your student's right side (fig. 5.5). This might be particularly painful, since the emotional energy stuck on the liver tends to rise and get stuck in the rib bones.

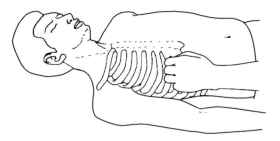

Fig 5.5. Work on the ribs with the knuckles.

◉ Releasing Wind from the Heart and Pericardium

The heart is the seat of emotions, and a lot of the blocked emotional energy is stored around that area. Assist your student in learning how to release the energy of emotions trapped in the chest by breathing deeply and smiling into the area. Making the heart sound (haw-w-w-w-w-w) as he or she exhales can help ease the pain. (See appendix 2 for more details.)

The pericardium is the sack around the heart that operates as the heart's heat exchanger and emergency heat vent. It helps to wick off the heart's excess energy. To increase the effectiveness of this approach, you can also guide your student to make the triple warmer's sound (hee-e-e-e-e-e), directing the vibration of the sound into the pericardium (see appendix 2). Feel love, feel soft; teach the student to smile. This will help cool the heart and prevent heart attacks. Encourage the student to practice every day for ten minutes.

When this wind exits, it leaves the heart and travels up the chest to the left shoulder and then down the left arm, to the fingernail of the little finger.

1. Begin by pressing your knuckle into points 22 and 23 on the left side. Point 22 is located right above the left nipple (fig. 5.6). For women, you can find the point above the left breast approximately between the fourth and fifth ribs, 1½ to 2 inches down from the collarbone. Point 23 is about an inch from point 22 toward the arm. These points are usually very sensitive. Use soft stimulation instead of a heavy pressure. Spiral the knuckle in a small area— a depression where the knuckle fits. Spiral counterclockwise to loosen.

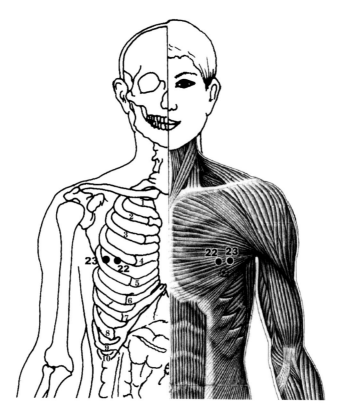

Fig. 5.6. Points on the chest

2. Flush the wind from the heart area by spiraling your hand above it counterclockwise and then moving your hand above the heart

meridian down the left arm. You will normally feel the dense, hot, or itchy energy leaving the heart, and you should direct it into the ground. The wind will flow out through the fingertips, especially the middle and pinky fingers. Your student can also focus on these fingers, exhaling out any excess heat from the pericardium and directing it toward the earth. The pericardium is like a cooling system for the heart.

3. Check the right side of the chest. Although wind trapped on this side does not affect the heart as much, if you do not release it this wind can later move into the left side. Work on points 22 and 23 on this side, and then flush the wind out through the right hand.

4. With your knuckle, release the area of the sternum, massaging between the ribs and directly on the rib bones, especially on the area around the heart (fig. 5.7).

   For women, work around the breast, moving it to the side to work on the ribs under it. When you work on the sternum, be

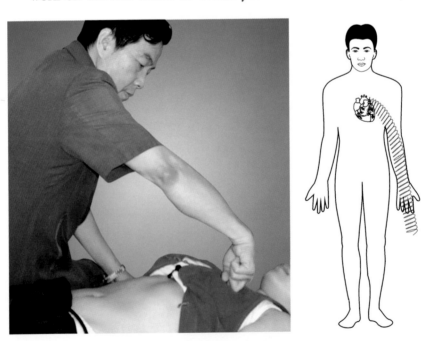

Fig. 5.7. Massage the sternum with the knuckles and vent the sick chi down and out of the left hand.

aware of how soft it is and do not press too hard. Usually, you will find the problem area close to the heart, and you may feel a kind of swelling like the surface of a balloon.

5. Flush the wind down from the left part of the chest through the left arm.

Note: If the chest area is too sensitive, use the tip of your finger instead of the knuckle.

⟳ Releasing Wind through the Knee Point

1. To find the related knee point 53, lay the palm of your hand on the midline directly over your student's knee. Your extended index finger should just about touch the gap above the kneecap. You will find the point as you extend your thumb to the inside of the leg and grab the inner thigh muscle (fig. 5.8). Massage the knee point.
2. Flush the wind down.
3. Repeat on the other leg.

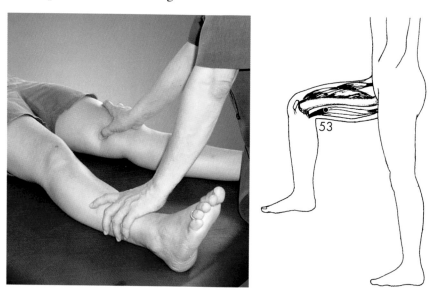

Fig. 5.8. Point 53 near the knee

 ## The Second Wind

Wind That Attacks the Tongue, Jaw, Eyes, and Head

The treatment for this wind is the continuation of the work for the first wind (fig. 5.9). The wind that attacks the liver and the heart is hot, so it tends to rise to the throat, paralyzing the root of the tongue and then affecting the jaw, the eyes, and the head. This wind can also impact the central nervous system. This is what often happens during heart attacks when people cannot speak. This wind often comes up when people are very angry, tense, or under a lot of stress. The treatment is also useful when the student is very emotional or has low self-esteem.

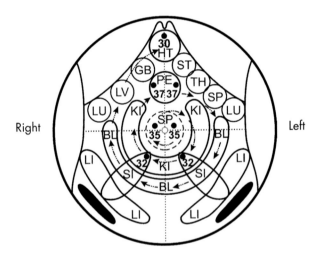

Fig. 5.9. Navel points for the second wind are the same as for the first wind.

Releasing Wind through the Chin

1. Release the root of the tongue by massaging the soft area under the chin.
2. Press point 15 under the chin, and then slowly slide the pads of your thumbs along the jawbone toward the back of the jaw and

then to the front again. Dig your thumbs in behind and against the bone (fig. 5.10). This place can accumulate a lot of emotions and it can be very painful. Repeat this 9 to 18 times. This procedure can release the tongue after a heart attack when there are speech problems.

3. Flush the winds down your student's arms.

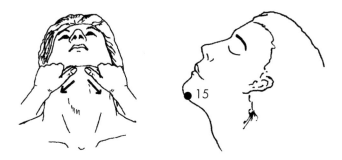

Fig. 5.10. Releasing the chin area

❷ *Releasing Wind through the Jaw*

When this wind is present, the jaw becomes tense and tight and there is often a history of nightmares. The people affected by it normally clench the jaw or grind the teeth, especially during the night. Over a series of sessions, the jaw can be released and TMJ syndrome (pain and tightness in the temporomandibular joint) may be relieved.

Liver excess is often the cause of this condition. It is important to release the toxins and wind in the liver as explained for the first wind before working directly on the jaw. Otherwise, the wind will rise from the liver, and the problems will manifest once again.

1. Ask your student to gently tighten and loosen her jaw by clenching her teeth. This allows you to find the muscle between the upper and lower jaw (fig. 5.11).

 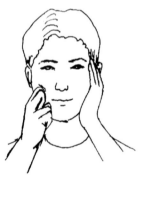

Fig. 5.11. Massaging the muscle between the upper and lower jaw

2. Supporting the face with your other hand, massage the muscle as your student repeatedly opens the jaw. This point can be very painful. Work on both sides of the jaw until you feel the tense

muscles easing. You can work on each side separately or on both sides simultaneously.

3. Use your knuckle or finger to press point 13 located right below the earlobe on the edge of the jaw (fig. 5.12). Work on both sides.

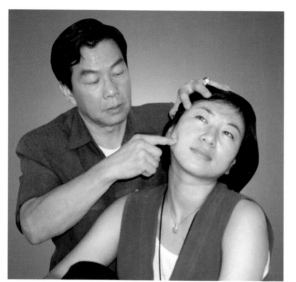 

Fig. 5.12. Pressing point 13 with the finger

4. As you work, ask your student to do the liver's sound (sh-h-h-h-h-h-h) subvocally, to facilitate the release of the wind (see appendix 2).

✪ Releasing Wind from the Head and Eyes

Use your knuckle to massage the following points on the face, spiraling in a tiny circle (see fig. 5.13 on page 62). These points are particularly powerful antidotes to migraine headaches and sore eyes or eye aches. Use the point of the knuckle at a 90-degree angle to the face or head.

1. Massage point 2 in the front of the skull on the center line above the hairline.

2. Massage point 3 on the area in the middle of the forehead.

3. Massage point 4 on the mid brow.

4. Massage point 5 above the middle of each eyebrow where you find a small notch.

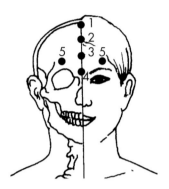

Fig. 5.13. Use your knuckles to massage points on the face and head.
Point 3 is being massaged in the photograph.

5. With your thumb, release the area all around the upper eye socket following the bone. Work slowly and softly from the inside to the outer edge (fig. 5.14). This can also relieve the heat, redness,

pain, and dryness in the eyes caused by liver wind. This massage is very effective with the swollen eyes that often come with migraine headaches.

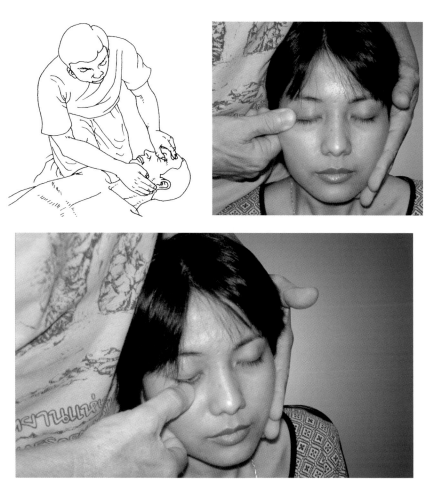

Fig. 5.14. Massaging the eye socket

6. Guide the student to turn her head to the opposite side from where you will work, and support the head with your other hand. Find point 10 on the temple just beyond the orbital bone on the outer edge of the eye (see fig. 5.15 on page 64). It will feel like a hole, valley, or indentation. Begin by releasing it gently with your

fingers, and then slowly and carefully insert your knuckle. Spiral following the student's exhalation. Work on the other side, and then do both sides simultaneously.

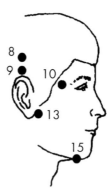

Fig. 5.15. Points 8, 9, 10, 13, and 15

7. The next points, 8 and 9, are located directly above the apex and on the centerline of each ear. Use your knuckle to massage each point individually and then both sides simultaneously (fig. 5.16).
8. Flush the wind out through your student's arms.

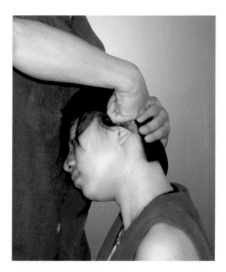

Fig. 5.16. Massaging point 8 above the ear

❂ *Releasing Wind through the Back of the Head*

1. Massage point 27 (Wind Pond) with your knuckle (fig. 5.17). To find it, search for an indentation on each side of the centerline area in the back of the neck above the base of the skull, about 1 inch above the bottom of the hairline. You will know you found the right "valley" spot when you can spiral with your knuckle without sliding or slipping out of the point.

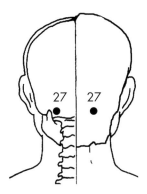

Fig. 5.17. Point 27

2. Find the curlicue, the spot (or spots, if there are more than one) where the hair spirals, and massage it with your knuckle, releasing any wind or stagnant chi that is blocked there.
3. Often, it is possible to feel the wind exiting the skull at this point. Gather it by swirling your hands above the head, and then direct the wind down the arms, out the hands, and into the earth.

To assist your student in moving to daily self-care, you can teach the points on the face so that she can work on them daily, particularly when the tense or painful condition is present.

The Third Wind

Wind That Attacks the Kidneys

This wind is caused by improper eating habits, such as eating too much cold-producing food (e.g., very cold drinks, unripe fruits, ice cream, and frozen or cold food right out of the refrigerator) and not chewing properly. It always starts from the small intestines, rising to the kidneys, moving up above the ears, and accumulating in the head. When this wind gets stuck in the brain, it can attack the nerves, causing the eyes to shake and making the teeth ache.

The small intestines are located over the kidneys. Excessive cold energy contracts the kidneys and makes the psoas muscles spasm and pull the spine toward the thighs (fig. 5.18). This stops the flow of energy and causes back pain. Bringing the excess heat from the heart down to the psoas muscles and kidneys relaxes and warms the lower back.

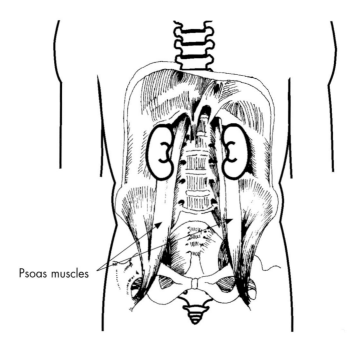

Psoas muscles

Fig. 5.18. The psoas muscles

Balancing the fire and water elements in the body (heat and cold) creates harmony throughout the entire system. Teach your student the Lotus meditation, to use the fire energy in the heart to warm the kidneys, and the cold water energy of the kidneys and earth to reduce excess heat in the heart. Just the right amount and flow of water and fire energy in the body will help to transform the accumulated stress in the mind and body into a sense of well-being.

❂ The Lotus Meditation

Imagine the heart as a red lotus flower and the pericardium (the heat-regulating membrane that encloses the heart) as the lotus pads. Visualize the kidneys as bulbs similar to the clusters or plexuses where the stems of the lotus pads and the lotus flower join together. In a pond or pool, there are usually several lotus plants that join together in a cluster, rooting in the mud. From the kidneys (kidney bulbs/ clusters), visualize roots extending down through the legs into the watery mud of the earth basin (see fig. 5.19 on page 68).

Through this dreamscape imagery of the body and the lotus merging in nature, sense these qualities of energy in your body. Feel the supporting connection with the same qualities of red and golden energy coming to us from the sun and the universe above, as well as the blue water energy coming from the earth and nature. Feel the warm red energy of the heart together with the red and yellow/gold from above. Likewise, sense the cool, blue water energy of the kidneys together with the refreshing blue water energy from the earth.

1. Breathing deeply into the lower abdomen, visualize your heart as a red lotus flower, your kidneys as its roots, and your spine as the stem that connects them.
2. Feel the roots of the lotus extending into the bed of the pond, absorbing the right amount of nutrition from the wet earth. Visualize the flower opening to the sun to receive its (fire) energy. Feel the healthy and supple spine as the stem connecting the two

Fig. 5.19. Lotus/heart/kidney energy dreamscape

energies. Feel the harmony of fire and water, yang and yin, male and female.

3. Inhale into the heart, drawing the warmth from the sun and feeling it come down through the crown of the head, and blend it with the love, joy, and happiness in the heart (red lotus). Draw this loving, hot heart energy back to the point opposite the heart in the center of the spine—the point between the scapulae, between T5 and T6—as you slowly inhale (fig. 5.20). Then, using the heart's sound (haw-w-w-w-w), exhale the hot energy down the spine (lotus stem) to the cool kidneys, warming them and warming the psoas muscles with the loving heat from the heart.

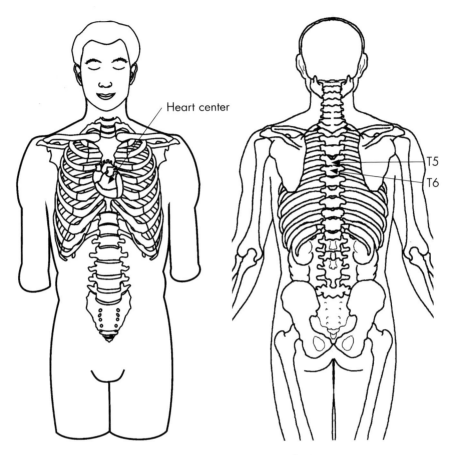

Fig. 5.20. Heart center, T5 and T6

4. See the kidneys as the nourishing bulbs of the lotus with roots that extend down through the legs to the soles of the feet, accessing the soothing blue water energy held by the earth.

5. Inhale into the kidneys, feeling the roots of the lotus extend down through the legs to the soles of the feet. With your inhalation, draw the cool, soothing, nourishing blue water energy through the soles of the feet, up through the legs to the kidneys. Feel the gentle, calm, peaceful energy of the kidneys blending with the cool, soothing blue water energy that has come up through the legs. Breathe out with the kidney sound, choo-oo-oo-oo. As you

exhale, send this energy up through the spine (stem) via the Wind Point to the heart.

6. Alternate inhaling into the heart and into the kidneys in this way for a few times.

7. Relax, breathe normally, and move your mind back and forth between the heart and kidneys along the connecting spinal stem. Smile with gratitude to your kidneys, spine, and heart.

For a more detailed description of the Lotus meditation, refer to *Energy Balance through the Tao* (Rochester, Vt.: Destiny Books, 2005).

◐ Pressing the Navel Points for the Third Wind

Loosen the small intestines. As you work with your elbow on your student's navel, he may complain of neck pain as the wind moves. Use your elbow to press the navel points for the third wind (fig. 5.21). These are not such exact points. It's more of a general area—wherever you find tension, a lump, stress. Hold the elbow there until the tension loosens. Feel the elbow inside the abdomen, and pay attention to the expression on the student's face. Remember to flush out the wind after pressing each point.

1. Press point 35, located just above the navel, on the left side.
2. Press point 33, located just below the navel, on the left side.
3. Press point 33 on the right side.
4. Press point 35 on the right side.
5. Press point 38, located to side of your student's navel, on the left side. This point relieves the wind that causes back pain.
6. Press point 32, located below the navel toward the outside of the body, on the left side.
7. Press point 32 on the right side.
8. Press point 38 on the right side.
9. Press point 36, located above the navel slightly toward the side of the body, on the right side.

10. Press point 36 on the left side.

11. Flush out through the knee point 53. Sometimes sick energy gets stuck at point 53 on the leg, so loosen up this point after working on the navel points.

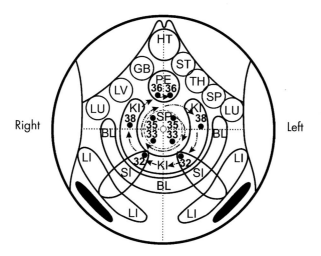

Fig. 5.21. Navel points for the third wind

⊙ Releasing Kidney Wind with the Head Point

1. Press point 8 with your knuckle, supporting the head with your other hand. This point is located in an indentation about one finger width above the tip of the ear (fig. 5.22). Work on both sides.

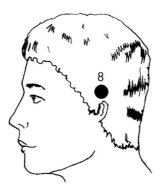

Fig. 5.22. Point 8 on the head

2. Instead of venting excess hot energy out through the arms and fingers, bring the excess heat of the heart down to the kidneys. When we bring excess heat down from the heart, heat from the head goes down also.

◉ Releasing Kidney Wind through the Knee Point

1. As described earlier, find the related knee point 53 by laying the palm of your hand on the midline directly over your student's knee. Your extended index finger should just about touch the gap above the kneecap. You will find the point as you extend your thumb to the inside of the leg and grab the inner thigh muscle (fig. 5.23). Massage the point with your thumb or knuckle.
2. Flush the wind out.
3. Repeat on the other leg.

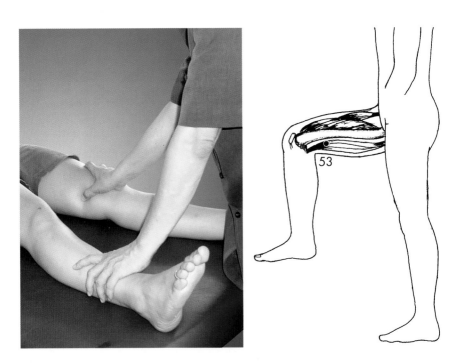

Fig. 5.23. Point 53 near the knee

The Fourth Wind

Wind That Causes Aches, Tightness, Tiredness, and Uneasiness in the Whole Body and Attacks the Vena Cava, Aorta, and Lumbar Plexus

The fourth wind causes a feeling of fatigue, aching, tightness, and uneasiness all over the body. This wind arises from too much acidity in the body. Excess acidity in the body will cause an exacerbated mucus production that can host excessive bacteria and viruses and will congest the organs. Acidity also affects the connective tissues, cartilage, and tendons, and it makes the bile duct constrict. Excess alkalinity, on the other hand (too much honey, too many sweet fruits or vegetables), overstresses the pancreas, so it is important to keep a balance in the body's pH by eating properly. (See Winds Generated by Food in chapter 1.) The unbalanced individual must change both the eating habits and the emotional habits. Mental stress and emotional distress are a main cause of an acidic metabolism because of the overproduction of stress hormones such as adrenaline and insulin, which are acidic and flood the entire system.

This wind also attacks the heart, causing pain and heartburn. When this wind activates, it reaches the heart area and comes up to the left shoulder and down the arm along the pericardium meridian. When this wind attacks the lumbar plexus, it spreads throughout the whole nervous system. Abdominal breathing and belching to loosen up stuck chi greatly helps to relieve this wind.

Pressing the Navel Points for the Fourth Wind

Use your elbow to press the navel points for the fourth wind (see fig. 5.24 on page 74). Find the tension, and then hold that point with the elbow until the tension is released and the winds go out. Flush out the wind after pressing each point. Talk to the winds and send them out to a better home—the earth!

Fig. 5.24. Navel points for the fourth wind

1. First press point 32, located just below the navel toward the outside of the body, on the left side.
2. Follow with point 32 on the right side.
3. Press point 41, located on the lower tip of the hip bone, on the right side.
4. Then press point 40, located right above the hip bone, on the right side.
5. Follow with point 40 on the left side.
6. Then press point 41 on the left side.
7. Press point 48, located on the front of the leg at the level of the sexual organs toward the inner thigh, on the left side. Use the tip of your fingers for this point (fig. 5.25).
8. Follow with point 48 on the right side.

◑ Releasing Wind from the Chest and Shoulders

Working on the chest and shoulders, we find many nerves. Respect the nerves by holding still—do not "monkey around" with the nerves.

This wind most often affects the left side only. All of the points described next refer to the left and right sides of the body; if the wind moves to the right side, you must also work on the same points on the right side of the body. Usually you do have to work on both sides.

1. With the student lying on her back, use your fingers to massage point 21 located below the collarbone and in the area above the left breast (see fig. 5.25). The heart and pericardium meridians both leave the heart and traverse the upper chest, going up to the shoulder and down the left arm.

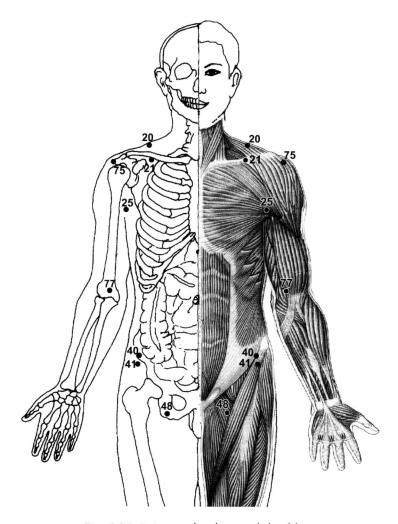

Fig. 5.25. Points on the chest and shoulders

2. Have your student sit up or turn on her side. With your elbow, press point 20 located above the clavicle, close to the neck (see fig. 5.53 on page 101).

3. Pinch the trapezius muscle on the area where the neck meets the shoulder. Pull it up and shake it, massaging the muscle and the nerves underneath to release the area.

4. Massage point 75, located on the outer edge of the shoulder, in the depression in the middle of the deltoid muscle (fig. 5.26). Raise the arm slowly so that the arm is horizontal.

Fig. 5.26. Massaging point 75

5. Massage point 25 in the student's left armpit (fig. 5.27). Have the student raise the arm slowly straight up as you press and find the point. The student leans into your thumbs.

6. Use your fingers to massage the Heart meridian all the way down the inside of your student's arm, pressing point 77 on the inner elbow as you go down (fig. 5.28).

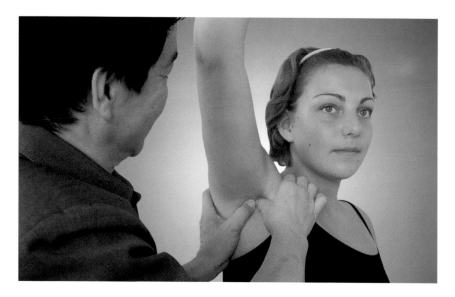

Fig. 5.27. Massaging point 25 with both thumbs

7. Continue massaging the arm down to the tip of the little finger. Pinch the end corners of the fingernail (see fig. 5.28).
8. Flush the winds down the left arm.

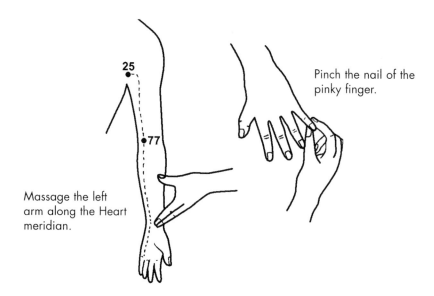

25

Pinch the nail of the pinky finger.

●77

Massage the left arm along the Heart meridian.

Fig. 5.28. Heart meridian

✿ *Working with Points on the Legs*

1. Press point 54 or point 69, located behind the kneecap (fig. 5.29).
2. Work on point 55, located on the inner part of the leg below the knee joint (fig. 5.30).
3. Work on Point 66 directly below the anklebone on the inside of the foot. Press down with both thumbs.
4. Flush the wind down the legs.

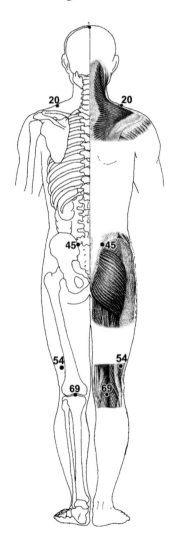

Fig. 5.29. Points 54, 69, and 45

🌀 Working with Points on the Back

1. Ask your student to turn so you can work on her back. Press your elbow on Point 45, in the space between the sacrum, Lumbar 5, and the hip bone (see fig. 5.29). Shake your arm and slightly push the hip bone down toward the buttocks to release the tension in that area (see fig. 5.57 page 106).

2. Flush the wind down the legs.

3. Remember to flush out the wind after pressing each Point 69 behind the knees.

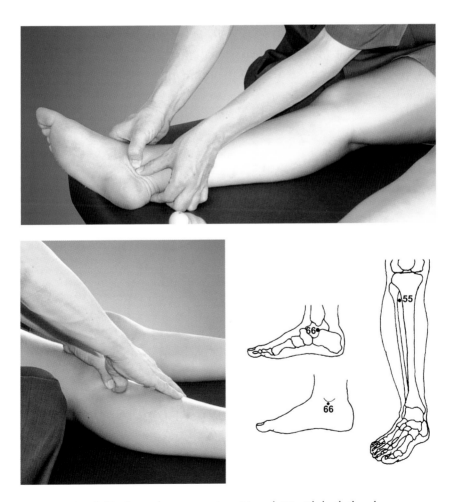

Fig. 5.30. Press down on points 66 and 55 with both thumbs.

The Fifth Wind

Wind That Makes the Abdomen Stiff, Hard, Tight, and Tender

This wind originates in the small intestine and causes shooting pains as it travels along the liver meridian. The upper right side of the abdomen will probably be bloated. This wind is caused by food and emotions, and it always starts in the intestines. It must first be removed from the small intestine and then from the liver (fig. 5.31).

When the intestines are bloated with wind, you must first work to clear the large intestine, then the small intestine, the liver, and the gallbladder, with the techniques presented in the first Chi Nei Tsang book. When you sense the knots and tangles releasing, use your elbows.

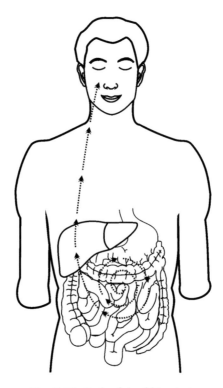

Fig. 5.31. Path of the fifth wind

🌀 Pressing the Navel Points for the Fifth Wind

Use your elbow to press the navel points for the fifth wind (fig. 5.32).
Remember to flush out the wind after pressing each point.

1. Press point 35 on the left side.
2. Press point 33, located just below the navel, on the left side.
3. Press point 33 on the right side.
4. Work on point 35, located just above the navel, on the right side.
5. Press point 36, located above the navel slightly toward the side of
   the body, on the right side.
6. Press point 36 on the left side.
7. Press point 41, located on the lower tip of the hip bone, on the left
   side.
8. Press point 41 on the right side.

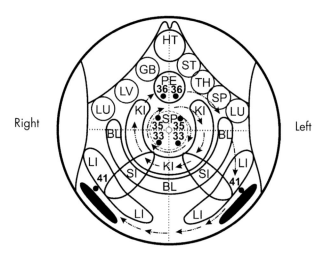

Fig. 5.32. Navel points for the fifth wind

⊙ Releasing Wind through the Crown and Perineum

1. With your knuckle, press on the Crown point 1, on the intersection of the lines drawn between the highest point of the ear and the midline of the nose. As you press this point, guide your student to connect with and lightly contract the perineum. Or put the knuckle in point 1 and spiral and hold, spiral and hold while the student holds and presses point 43 with the middle fingers (fig. 5.33).

2. Press CNT point 43 (Hui Yin), or have your student press it himself. It is a good idea to cover students with a sheet or a towel across the genitals so they have a sense of privacy when working on this delicate point. Coach your student to contract his mouth and suck the lips until they are tightly pursed and contract the anus by sensing and pulling up on the front, back, middle, left, and right parts of the anus. Hui Yin is where all yin and sick energy gathers.

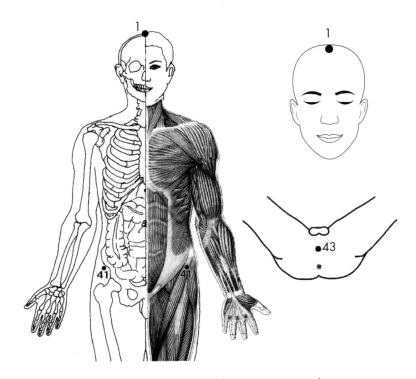

Fig. 5.33. Points on the inguinal area, crown, and perineum

3. Flush and vent from the head down the arms and out; flush and vent from point 43 down and out the legs.

4. Encourage your student to massage the perineum at home daily while practicing the anus contraction exercises and touching the crown of the head for as long as the symptoms of tightness in the abdomen persist.

⊘ Working with Points on the Legs

1. Press point 57, located on the inner part of the leg below the knee joint, with the elbow or thumbs. You can use a little oil here (fig. 5.34).

2. Work on point 66 directly below the anklebone on the inside of the foot. Use the thumbs to push down and out.

3. Flush the wind down the legs.

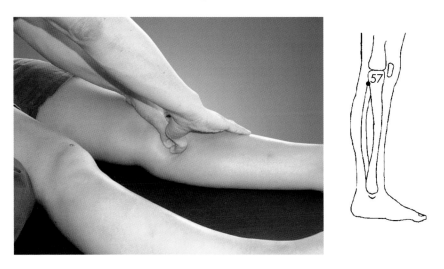

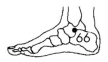

Fig. 5.34. Points on the legs and feet

The Sixth Wind

Wind That Causes Cramps

This wind causes cramps and tightness in the legs, the back, and the neck. The cramps usually start in the abdomen but they attack the nervous system and the muscles. When this wind is present, there is a lot of stiffness and pain.

The cramps created by this wind result from problems with the flow of blood that returns to the heart when the veins, especially the vena cava, are congested. For instance, when this wind is present, if the legs get too cold and the muscles contract, the flow of blood is obstructed and this causes cramps. Releasing the wind relieves the swelling and restores the proper flow of blood.

⚙ *Pressing the Navel Points for the Sixth Wind*

Use your elbow to press the navel points for the sixth wind (fig. 5.35). Remember to flush out the wind after pressing each point.

1. Press point 35 on the left side.
2. Press point 33, located just below the navel, on the left side.

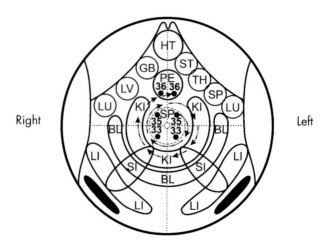

Fig. 5.35. Navel points for the sixth wind

3. Press point 33 on the right side.
4. Press point 35, located just above the navel, on the right side.
5. Press point 36, located above the navel slightly toward the side of the body, on the right side.
6. Press point 36 on the left side.

⊙ Working with Points on the Face

1. Press point 15 in the depression under the chin behind the lower jaw with your thumb (fig. 5.36). Press up toward the tongue.
2. Press your knuckle into point 13, located right below the earlobe on the edge of the jaw (fig. 5.36). You may work on each side separately or on both sides simultaneously.
3. Flush the sick energy out through the arms.

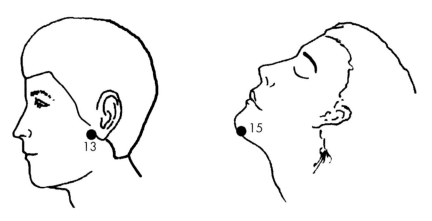

Fig. 5.36. Points on the face

⊙ Releasing Wind through the Legs

1. Stretch you student's calves and Achilles' tendons by pushing his feet toward the navel and moving the feet circularly, maintaining tension on the calf muscles (see fig. 5.37 on page 86).
2. Flush the wind down.

3. Ask your student to turn over. With your elbow, work on point 69 on the back of the knees, in the split of the muscle below the knee (fig. 5.38).

Fig. 5.37. Stretching the calves

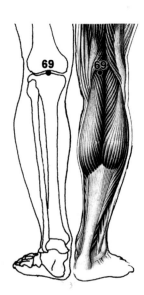

Fig. 5.38. Point on the legs

4. Flush the wind down the legs.

5. Your student should continue the work at home by pulling her toes back toward the navel, and extending the heels until the legs are tight, then releasing and exhaling. Standing on the toes, and then rocking back to the heels and lifting the toes, can help relieve congestion by encouraging the flow of blood into the calf muscles.

◎ Slapping Technique

This technique relieves the stagnation behind the knees, elbows, and other joints, such as the inside of the ankles and the wrists (fig. 5.39). Be careful *not* to work on varicose veins. Afterward, the slapped area should not be touched.

Fig. 5.39. Slapping technique

1. Support the extended leg, arm, wrist, or ankle with just a bit of slack in the joint. With the open palm, strike the back of the joint quickly. It may cause a sharp, stinging sensation and may even

cause a bit of welting and redness, which will dissipate as the stagnant blood is reabsorbed into the body. This technique can be painful, but it is very effective to stimulate and restore the free flow of clean, healthy, oxygenated blood into the joints. Tell the student to not take a shower or wet the area for 12 hours.

2. Flush the wind down.

3. After the treatment, your student should do monkey dancing (fig. 5.40). Lying on his back, he should raise arms and legs toward the ceiling and shake them while breathing deeply into the abdomen. This helps blood circulation and lymph flow. This is a daily practice to get stagnant blood moving.

4. Ask your student to do deep belly laughing. Also known as "beating the inner drum," it will help your student as it pumps the abdomen, activating the flow of blood, lymph, and chi, and massaging all the internal organs.

Fig. 5.40. Monkey dancing

The Seventh Wind

Wind That Attacks the Heart Causing Shaking

This wind starts in the intestines and attacks the heart as it rises. When the heart overheats, the jaws tighten, the whole body may shake, and in extreme cases, the body becomes paralyzed. This is sometimes misdiagnosed as Parkinson's disease. The intestines cover a broad area; when this wind is high and centered in the intestines, it attacks the heart directly. Working on this wind also helps to relieve back pain.

The right amount and flow of water and fire energy in the body is very important. In nature, too much cold makes it impossible for anything to live, while too much heat burns everything up. Balance creates a sense of well-being.

☁ *Navel Points for the Seventh Wind*

Use your elbow to press the navel points for the seventh wind (fig. 5.41). Remember to flush out the wind after pressing each point.

1. Press point 35, located just above the navel, on the left side.
2. Press point 33, located just below the navel, on the left side.

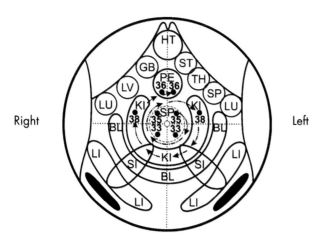

Fig. 5.41. Navel points for the seventh wind

3. Press point 33 on the right side.
4. Press point 35 on the right side.
5. Press point 38, located to the side of the navel, on the left side.
6. Press point 38 on the right side.
7. Press point 36, located above the navel slightly toward the side of the body, on the right side.
8. Press point 36 on the left side.

❷ Releasing Wind through the Face

1. With your knuckle, press point 13, located below the ear toward the end of the jawbone, while supporting the face with the other hand (fig. 5.42).
2. Flush the energy out through the arms.

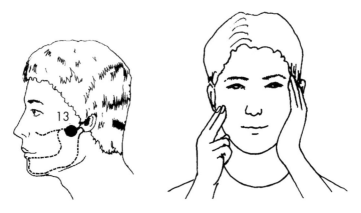

Fig. 5.42. Point 13 on the face

❷ Balancing Fire and Water Energy through the Feet

"Keep on digging the soles of the feet and you'll find gold."

1. Press point 74 (Bubbling Spring), located on the soles of the feet at one-third of the distance from the base of the second toe to the

heel (fig. 5.43). As you stimulate the point, guide your student to pull the tips of her toes toward the navel as she inhales, bringing the cold, refreshing energy of the kidneys from this point at the beginning of the Kidney meridian. Ask her to feel the energy going up through the insides of the legs, then through the back of the perineum, up into the lower abdomen, wrapping the kidneys and the adrenal glands, and rising all the way up to the heart area just under the collarbones (see fig. 5.44 on page 92).

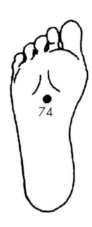

Fig. 5.43. Bubbling Spring point

2. As you flush the wind out through the feet, ask your student to exhale, while doing the heart sound (haw-w-w-w-w-w), any excess heat from the heart down to the kidneys, then through the back and legs, and out through the toes into the earth (see fig. 5.44 on page 92). The shaking should start to lessen immediately. The Lotus meditation we described in the Third Wind practice is also very helpful in this case, as it uses the cold, water energy of the kidneys to reduce excess heat in the heart.

3. Encourage swallowing saliva and frequent belching. This cools the heart down and moisturizes the overheated organs.

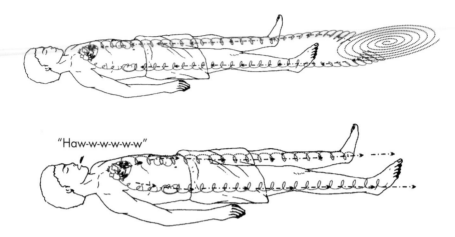

Fig. 5.44. Draw cool refreshing kidney energy in through the soles of the feet. Exhale out the excess heat with the heart sound.

The Eighth Wind

Wind That Causes Chest Pain

This wind causes pain in the chest and back as well as allergic rashes. It rises as a result of excess mucus sticking to the veins and arteries. The lower abdomen often feels like it has jelly inside. The body creates an excessive amount of mucus when it is too acidic, so it is important for the student to eat a greater amount of alkaline foods. (Refer to Winds Generated by Food in chapter 1.) Chewing food well and mixing it with saliva promotes good digestion and avoids the problems created by this wind. You should chew so much that you end up "drinking your food."

Tell your student to try counting how many times she normally chews a mouthful; then, to chew many more times, until the solid food becomes liquid. The student should also avoid eating foods to which she is allergic and, if possible, avoid areas where the air pollution is too strong or the pollen is too highly concentrated, if this affects her system. Adjusting the acidity and alkalinity of the diet and cleaning out the colon will render deep results. To rid the body of excess mucus, students can also learn to drink their own fresh urine. (See the book *Urine Therapy*, by Flora Peschek-Böhmer and Gisela Schreiber.*)

◎ Navel Points for the Eighth Wind

Use your elbow to press the navel points for the eighth wind (fig. 5.45). Remember to flush out the wind after pressing each point.

1. Press point 35, located just above the navel, on the left side.
2. Press point 33, located just below the navel, on the left side. This point (together with point 38) is good for relieving back pain.

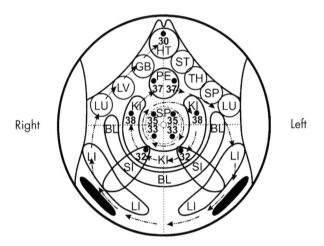

Fig. 5.45. Navel points for the eighth wind

3. Press point 33 on the right side.
4. Press point 35 on the right side.
5. Press point 38, located to side of your student's navel, on the left side.

---

*Flora Peschek-Böhmer and Gisela Schreiber, *Urine Therapy* (Rochester, Vt.: Healing Arts Press, 1999).

6. Press point 32, located below the navel toward the outside of the body, on the left side.
7. Press point 32 on the right side.
8. Press point 38 on the right side.
9. Press point 37, located on a line right above the navel, on the right side.
10. Press point 37 on the left side.
11. Press point 30, located below the lower end of the sternum. Be careful not to press on the tip of the sternum, as it is very delicate.

☯ Releasing Wind from the Chest

1. Massage the whole chest area. Use the heel of the palm to loosen the entire rib cage (fig. 5.46). Keep the palm in one place and vigorously spiral and shake. Now work your knuckle between the ribs and right on the rib bones using one hand to hold the rib cage. For women, work around the breast, moving it to the side to work on the ribs under it. The chest area may be very painful due to the great number of emotions (anger, sadness, jealousy, depression, etc.) stored there. Tell your student to keep breathing into the area so that the pain and the emotions can be released.

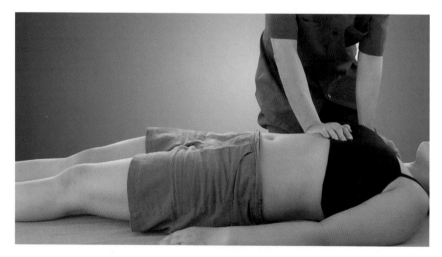

Fig. 5.46. Loosen the rib cage by shaking it with the heel of the hand.

2. Work on the sternum with your knuckle (fig. 5.47). Be aware of the tip of the sternum, how soft it is, and do not press too hard.
3. Flush the wind down through the arms.

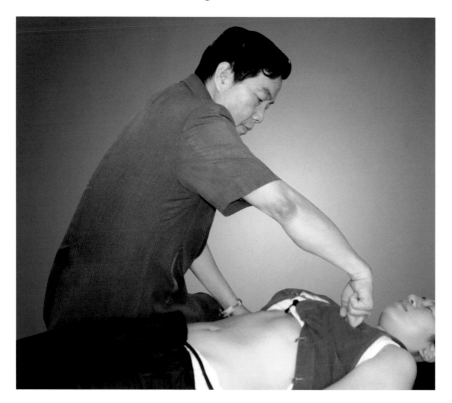

Fig. 5.47. Massage the sternum with the knuckle.

 The Ninth Wind

Wind That Makes the Legs and Feet Tired

This wind causes a lot of pain and fatigue in the legs and feet. When the legs are tired, winds often accumulate in the chest and abdomen, straining the organs and the psoas muscle. When the psoas muscle is tight, it pulls the lower back and the pelvis into painful misalignment. Over time, the muscles are unable to move back into a natural position.

☸ Navel Points for the Ninth Wind

Use your elbow to press the navel points for the ninth wind (fig. 5.48). Remember to flush out the wind after pressing each point.

1. Press point 35, located just above the navel, on the left side.
2. Press point 33, located just below the navel, on the left side.

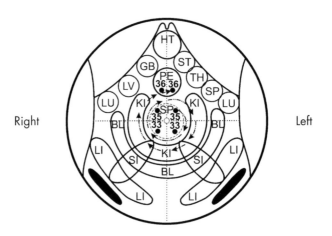

Fig 5.48. Navel points for the ninth wind

3. Press point 33 on the right side.
4. Press point 35 on the right side.
5. Press point 36, located above the navel slightly toward the side of the body, on the right side.
6. Press point 36 on the left side.

☸ Releasing Wind from the Chest

1. Press your knuckle into point 22, located right above the nipples (fig. 5.49). For women, you can find the point above the breasts approximately between the fourth and fifth ribs, 1½ to 2 inches down from the collarbone.

2. Do point 22 on the other side.

3. Flush the wind down the arms.

❂ Releasing Wind from the Inguinal Area

There are many blood vessels crossing this area. Working on these points helps to restore proper blood circulation and release the nerves. This area is very sensitive, so you should work gently with your elbow. Many people, especially women, have a lot of emotions and guilt stuck in the area under the navel and particularly in the groin. When the psoas muscles are in good shape, this region is not painful at all.

1. Press point 40 on the left side, located right above the hip bone (fig. 5.49).

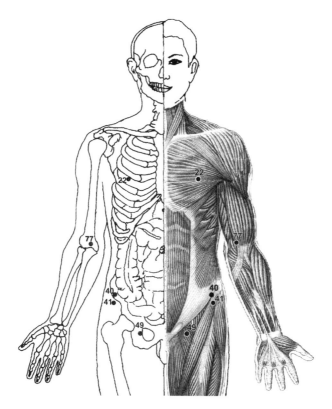

Fig. 5.49. Points on the chest and inguinal area

2. Press point 41 on the left side, located on the lower tip of the hip bone.

3. Press point 49, located just inside the lower part of the pelvic bone, on the left side. Ask permission to work on this point, and work very respectfully, since the area is very close to the pubic bone and thus close to the sexual organs. If your student becomes aroused, help him guide the energy up through the Microcosmic Orbit.

4. Press point 49 on the right side.

5. Press point 41 on the right side.

6. Press point 40 on the right side.

7. Flush the winds down through the legs.

❋ Working with Points on the Legs

The following points should be pressed with the tips of the fingers.

1. Work on point 63 located right above the anklebone on the inner side of the leg (fig. 5.50).

2. Work on point 66, located directly below the anklebone on the inside of the foot.

3. Work on point 55, located in the front of the leg under the knee between the two bones (see fig. 5.30, page 79).

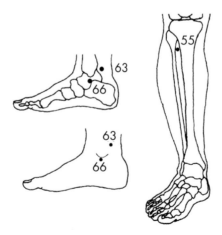

Fig. 5.50. Points on the legs and feet

4. Work on the other leg.

5. Flush the wind down the legs.

The Tenth Wind

Wind That Causes Pain, Numbness, and Heat

This wind causes pain, numbness, and heat that extend from the legs up to the armpits and hands. The heat is felt rising upward, making it difficult to walk. Working on the center of the navel and the midline up to the sternum works for people with back pain. After 15–20 minutes, it is possible to create a release and restore the ability to walk. This wind also attacks the heart, so you will need to work on the upper chest as well.

Navel Points for the Tenth Wind

Use your elbow to press the navel points for the tenth wind (fig. 5.51). Remember to flush out the wind after pressing each point.

While working with these navel points, rest a finger on point 19 (see fig. 5.52 on page 100).

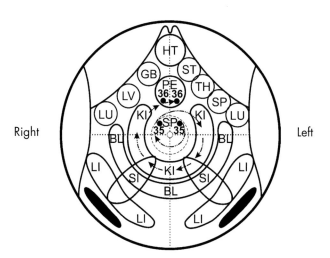

Fig. 5.51. Navel points for the tenth wind

1. Press point 35, located just above the navel, on the left side.
2. Press point 35 on the right side.
3. Press point 36, located above the navel slightly toward the side of the body, on the right side.
4. Press point 36 on the left side.

☯ Releasing Wind from the Chest and Throat

Releasing these points allows courage to grow.

1. Press your knuckle, or thumb, or finger on point 19, located between the collarbones where they join the sternum (fig. 5.52).
2. Work on points 18, located slightly above either side of point 19, right above the clavicle. There may be pain all over in this area. Work to release the tightness with your thumb and index finger.

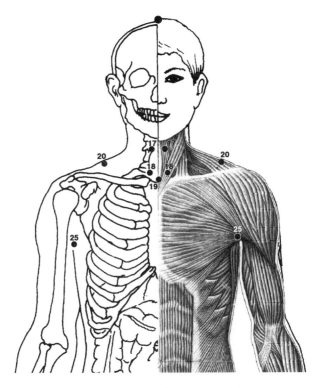

Fig. 5.52. Points on the chest and throat

Massage the entire area and directly over the left and right clavicle as well.

3. Massage and open point 17, located on the throat on the sides of the depression of the pharyngeal prominence, under the notch on both sides of the voicebox.

4. Flush the wind down through the arms.

✪ Working with Points on the Shoulders and Back

This is good for a stiff neck.

1. Press point 20 with your elbow, massaging the whole brachial plexus (fig. 5.53). Tell your student to slowly turn her head away from the side you are working on as you press down. Try a few drops of oil with this move.

2. With your thumb, press point 25 on the armpit (see fig. 5.27 on page 77).

3. Flush the wind out the arms.

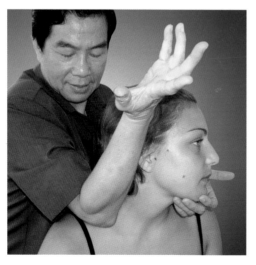
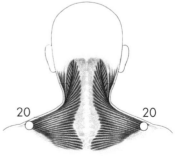

Fig. 5.53. Point 20, the shoulder well

⊙ *Working with Points on the Feet*

1. First use the two thumbs on points 66 and 67 (fig. 5.54). Then connect the navel with points 66 and 67 by placing the fingers of one hand on the navel while using the thumb to massage down from points 66 and 67.
2. Work on point 67, located on the inside of the foot below the anklebone toward the front.

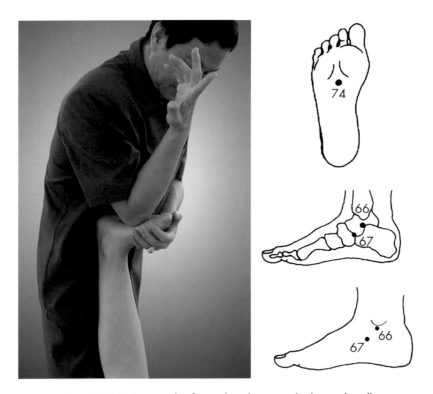

Fig. 5.54. Points on the feet—the photograph shows the elbow in the Bubbling Spring point.

3. Work on point 66 directly below the anklebone on the inside of the foot.
4. Supporting your student's foot with one hand, work on point 74, the Bubbling Spring point, on the sole of the foot located at one-

third of the distance from the base of the second toe to the heel. This point is like a well. When sick energy accumulates there, it can remain stagnant for a very long time.

5. Do the other foot.
6. Flush the wind out.

 ## The Eleventh Wind

Wind That Affects the Nerves and Makes the Back Stiff

This wind affects nearly everyone at one time or another. It collects directly below the navel and can cause a stiff back and affect the nerves and the lumbar plexus. Before you work on this wind, you must release the navel area and the psoas muscle with the basic Chi Nei Tsang procedure. (For a detailed procedure, refer to *Chi Nei Tsang*.)

Navel Points for the Eleventh Wind

Use your elbow to press the navel points for the eleventh wind (see fig. 5.55 on page 104). Remember to flush out the wind after pressing each point. Encourage your student to make the triple warmer sound, hee-e-e-e-e-e (see appendix 2), to assist in venting the winds.

1. Press point 35, located just above the navel, on the left side.
2. Press point 33, located just below the navel, on the left side.
3. Press point 33 on the right side.
4. Press point 35 on the right side.
5. Press point 38, located to the side of your student's navel, on the left side. This point relieves the wind that causes back pain.
6. Press point 32, located below the navel toward the outside of the body, on the left side.
7. Press point 32 on the right side.
8. Press point 38 on the right side.

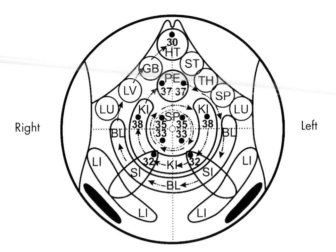

Fig. 5.55. Navel points for the eleventh wind

9. Press point 37, located on a line right above the navel, on the right side.

10. Press point 37 on the left side.

11. Press point 30, located below the lower end of the sternum. Be careful not to press on the tip of the sternum, as it is very delicate.

12. Conclude the massage work by gently using your fingers to massage the area just below the navel.

13. Finally, have the student place his palms over his lower abdomen and warm the area by imagining a fire or the sun burning in his abdomen. You may also directly introduce warming energy into this area with your intention and by sending wind-burning energy from your fingertips. Review this method ("Baking the Cold Wind") in the first Chi Nei Tsang book.

☾ Releasing Wind from the Shoulders

Sometimes before this wind exits the student's body it moves into areas where he is used to storing pain, such as the back, hips, or shoulders.

This is a good sign; it means the winds are moving. Help the student visualize the wind moving out through the legs and toes or through the arms and fingers.

1. Massage point 75, located on the outer edge of the shoulders in the depression in the middle of the deltoid muscle (fig. 5.56).
2. With your elbow, press point 20 on the shoulders at the base of the neck (see fig. 5.53 on page 101).
3. Flush the winds out through the arms.

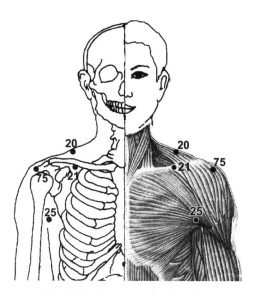

Fig. 5.56. Points on the shoulders

✪ Releasing Wind from the Back

1. Press your elbow on point 45, located in the space between the sacrum, Lumbar 5, and the hip bone (see fig. 5.57 on page 106). Shake your arm and slightly push the hip bone down toward the buttocks to release the tension in that area.
2. Flush the wind down through the legs and feet.

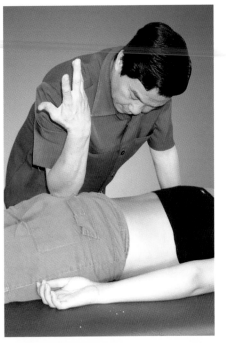
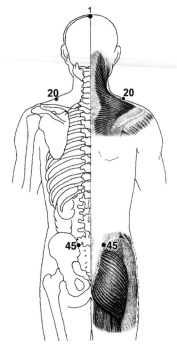

Fig. 5.57. Massaging point 45

The Twelfth Wind

Wind That Causes Excess Heat and Cold

Your student may complain of excess heat or cold or a rapid alternation of both hot and cold wind. Releasing excess cold and/or heat entails gathering the imbalanced wind and sweeping it out. The right temperature in the body provides a sense of well-being.

Excessive cold in the kidneys can be a cause of impotence. Erection of the penis is dependent on healthy chi flow. Venting excess heat from the heart helps to warm the kidneys, which must maintain a measure of internal heat to balance their innate coolness and function properly. This promotes the "yang within the yin" and an appropriate flow of chi. The Lotus meditation, described earlier in relation to the third wind, is very helpful to balance the cold and hot energies in the body.

Navel Points for the Twelfth Wind

Use your elbow to press the navel points for the twelfth wind (fig. 5.58). Remember to flush out the wind after pressing each point.

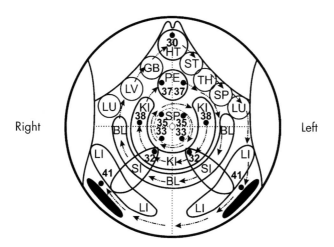

Fig. 5.58. Navel points for the twelfth wind

1. Press point 35, located just above the navel, on the left side.
2. Press point 33, located just below the navel, on the left side.
3. Press point 33 on the right side.
4. Press point 35 on the right side.
5. Press point 38 on the left side.
6. Press point 32 on the left side.
7. Press point 32 on the right side.
8. Press point 38 on the right side.
9. Press point 37, located on a line right above the navel, on the right side.
10. Press point 37 on the left side.
11. Press point 30, located below the lower end of the sternum. Be careful not to press on the tip of the sternum, as it is very delicate.
12. Press point 41, located on the lower tip of the hip bone, on the left side.
13. Press point 41 on the right side.

❃ Releasing Wind from the Chest

1. Check the upper part of the rib cage. Release the area on the sternum, between the ribs and directly on the rib bones (fig. 5.59). For

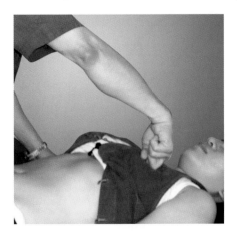
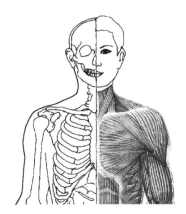

Fig. 5.59. Massaging the sternum

women, work around the breast, moving it to the side to work on the ribs under it. When you work on the sternum, be aware of how soft it is and do not press too hard.

2. As you work, coach your student to make the heart sound, haw-w-w-w-w (see appendix 2), and release any excess heat or cold through the feet.

3. Flush the wind down from the left part of the chest through the left arm, and from the right part of the chest through the right arm.

❂ *Releasing Wind through the Feet*

1. Supporting your student's foot with one hand, press your other elbow on the Bubbling Spring point, point 74, on the sole of the foot (fig. 5.60). Remember that this point is like a well, and any sick energy that accumulates there can remain stagnant for a very long time.

2. Flush down the wind.

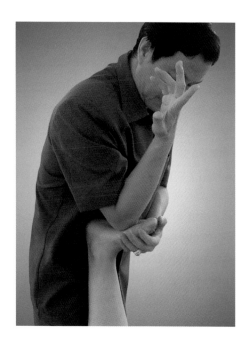 

Fig. 5.60. "Digging for gold" in the Bubbling Spring point

6

Applying Advanced Chi Nei Tsang to Specific Ailments

 ## Heart Attacks and the Life and Death Point

When a person is close to death, the heart begins to struggle. It balloons and expands until it collapses, and eventually the heart dies. If you find yourself in a situation where someone is having a heart attack, first call for an ambulance; then you can work on the person while you wait. You can help the person by using wind removal techniques (see the sections of chapter 5 on the first, third, seventh, and eleventh winds). You can also help by working on the "Life and Death point."

This point is located on the back, between the scapula and the spine, between Thoracic 4 and 6 on the left side (fig. 6.1). When a person is having a heart attack, this point is very clear as it pulses and pops out. It can be the size of a Ping-Pong ball. This point can also be used preventively. My master taught me this point when he was close to death—by working on it, I was able to extend his life.

The corresponding point on the right side is also important to work on, because there can be a reaction from the heart manifesting in that area also. So, in an emergency, the primary target area would be on the left where the skin first "pops out." Then, when you get the heart calmed down, you would also work on the right side to further relieve the pressure and balance the two sides. When it is not an emergency situation, you would work on both points preventively and for other health benefits.

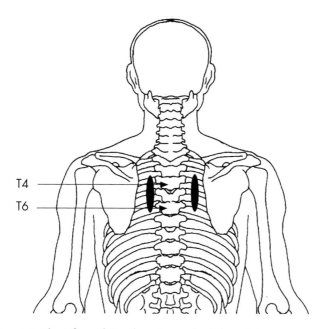

Fig. 6.1. The Life and Death point on the left and the corresponding point on the right

◉ *Procedure*

1. Stand behind the seated person; or if he is too weak to sit, lay him face down. If you are not using a massage table with a cut out for the face to rest in, place soft pillow rolls or pillows under the armpits and rest the forehead on another pillow.

2. The protruding point is easy to see and feel, especially if it is a strong heart attack and the person is gasping for breath. Applying pressure to this point with your thumb or knuckle will not be sufficient, so you must use your elbow to press and release, repeating

until the ball recedes. When the heart is weak, this area tends to be very sensitive.

3. Spiral with your hand above the area around the Life and Death point; direct the wind down the person's left arm and hand, and move it out of the body and into the ground.

When you are finished with the emergency technique, apply the following restorative technique.

1. You may chase out the wind that causes heart attacks by massaging the liver, then the gallbladder, the duodenum, and the small and large intestines. Review this technique in the first Chi Nei Tsang book. Pay special attention to the ileocecal valve at the end of the small intestine, in the lower right corner near the hip, as the wind can get stuck there (fig. 6.2).

2. Apply the technique for removing wind from the liver (see the section on the first wind in chapter 5).

3. Move the wind down the legs and feet and out of the body into the earth.

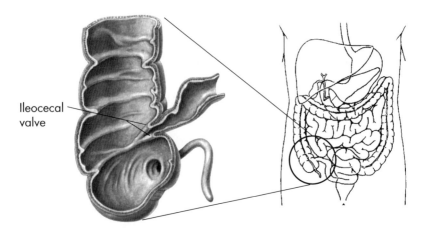

Ileocecal valve

Fig. 6.2. The ileocecal valve

Releasing Energy Blockages between the Heart, Kidneys, Ovaries, and Cervix and Restoring Milk Production in the Breasts

In women, energy often gets stuck on the heart area between T4 and T6. This blockage prevents the energy from reaching the nipples, the kidneys, the ovaries, and the cervix, causing problems with menstruation and impairing milk production in nursing mothers. Releasing the blockage restores the production of milk and alleviates menstrual problems.

If a mother is not breast-feeding her baby, the energy gets stuck in the chest area. With the following procedure, the unused milk can be turned into blood and then into chi. One of the main goals of the Universal Tao practice for women is to change blood energy into chi, since this energy is more useful and efficient.

◈ Procedure

1. Open the point located between the shoulder blade and the spine, between T4 and T6 directly behind the nipple, by pressing it with your knuckle (see fig. 6.3 on page 114).
2. Gather the stagnant chi by spiraling your hand over the area, and then sweep it down the arm and out through the hand.
3. Work on the other side.
4. Flush the wind down the arms.
5. Massage the area all around the top and sides of the pubic bone. The student should do this at home every day.
6. Flush the wind down the legs.

The following exercise is also helpful to free the points behind the heart.

Have your student lie comfortably on her back with her knees bent and her feet flat on the floor. Encourage her to raise her arms straight up in the air with the palms together (see fig. 6.4 on page 114). The pelvis should be tilted so that the small of the back is flat

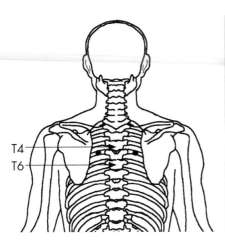
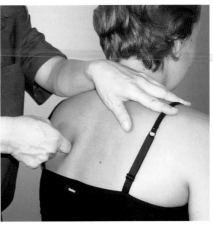

Fig. 6.3. Points between T4 and T6

against the floor. As she exhales, have her extend the fingertips to the sky and rotate the palms in a circle moving up and around. Stretch and reach the arms way up, lifting the shoulders off the mat. The scapulae must move. Then have her rest. Have her lower the hands until the scapulae are flat on the floor, and breathe long, silky breaths with her tongue on the roof of the mouth. Spiral energy at the heart, kidneys, and sexual organs, and exhale any cloudy, gray, or sick energy. This practice stimulates and opens T4 to T6 on the spine. It strengthens the heart-genital connection and helps to restore the flow of kidney and sexual energy to the nipples and reproductive organs.

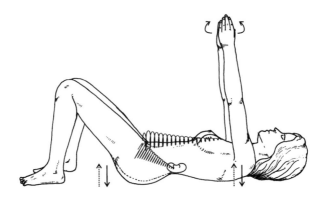

Fig. 6.4. Freeing up the Thoracic 4, 5, 6 area behind the heart.

Releasing Anger in the Jaw and Liver

It is important to release the toxins and wind in the liver before working directly on relieving the tension and wind in the jaw. Otherwise, the wind will again rise from the liver and affect the jaw. Many massage therapists ignore this (see the section on the second wind in chapter 5).

Procedure

1. Work on the student's right side. Use your knuckle to massage the area on the lowest ribs above the liver, pressing point 24.
2. Holding the head steady on the opposite side from where you will work, cup the fingers under the jaw and use your thumb to release point 13 (see fig. 5.42 on page 90).
3. Work on the opposite side of the student's jaw.

Arthritis

Arthritis is caused by the wind produced by stagnant and blocked blood. Normally, the blood runs up the veins in the legs and arms, collecting waste material and toxins on its way back to the heart. But sometimes, this toxic blood and wind collects in places like the back of the knees, the bend of the arm, or the lumbar area of the back, especially when people are too emotional, do not exercise enough, or eat heavy foods.

Procedure for Removing Wind from the Back of the Knees

1. The student should stand with the back of the knees bare. You should kneel to the side of the student as in fig. 6.5 on page 116.
2. Support the knee by holding it in the front with one hand. With the palm of the other hand, swiftly slap the back of each knee

about 9, 18, or 36 times, mobilizing your energy from your center (fig. 6.5). The hand action should be forceful, but not too hard. The skin on the back of the knees will be come quite flushed and the wind will reveal itself in ugly patches that will quickly turn a dark, reddish blue. The area will be bruised for a few days. This is a good sign that the winds have been stirred and activated, and they will now exit the body. If there is no wind trapped in this area, this reaction will not occur and the skin will just turn red temporarily.

3. Work on the other knee.

4. The student should not shower immediately after the treatment.

Fig. 6.5. Slapping technique

☯ Procedure for Removing Wind from the Middle Bend of the Arm

1. Both you and the student stand facing each other an arm's length apart, or you can stand beside the student (fig. 6.6).

2. Take the student's elbow and grip it. Slap the inside of the arm in the region of the crease in the elbow 18 times. The skin may become red and blotchy. You have stirred the winds and they will begin to leave the body, allowing better circulation in the area just treated.

3. Work on the other arm.

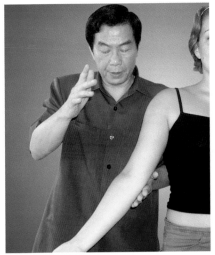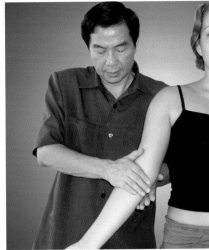

Fig. 6.6. Slap the inside of the arm.

If people have varicose veins in the back of the knees or elbows, you should only pat the area gently or wait for them to recede. Sometimes one leg is in better shape than the other, and working only on the "good" leg will also affect the other leg in a positive way.

Note: After performing this particular kind of wind removal, you should be careful to ground any negative energy you have transferred from the student to your hands.

Constipation

The wind stuck on the upper left side of the large intestines where the transverse and descending colon meet is powerful enough to stop all movement of the waste in the colon and can cause serious heart problems. Wind trapped in this area causes the large intestine to push up against the diaphragm, and the diaphragm to push up against the heart. This causes pain in the left arm and behind the left shoulder, and many people may erroneously think that they are having a heart attack. This pressure can also cause anxiety attacks.

Procedure

1. Open the wind gates with your elbow (see Opening the Wind Gates in chapter 4).
2. Release the intestines, focusing on the ileocecal valve and the transversal, descending, and sigmoid colon. (For a detailed explanation, refer to *Chi Nei Tsang*.)
3. Spiral and release the wind through the legs.
4. The student should continue to massage her abdomen every day.

Hiatal Hernia

Hiatal hernias are caused by the same wind that attacks the heart. This problem results from issues in the digestive system, compounded by excess weight and progressive weakening of the tissues in the abdomen.

Food that is not digested properly ferments inside the stomach, creating wind. The bloated stomach pushes against the diaphragm, and sometimes a part of the stomach may push through the hiatus— the opening in the diaphragm through which the esophagus and the two vagus nerves pass—enlarging and becoming a hernia (fig 6.7). Discomfort comes from the constant pressure of tissue pushing its way through the weakened hiatal opening. As more tissue pushes through the weakened area, the feeling of pressure increases. In addition, gastric acid is not contained in the stomach, and as it flows back into the esophagus, the person experiences a burning sensation and pain that extends all the way to the upper part of the chest. The congestion in the digestive tract also affects the heart, the liver, the spleen, and the lungs.

Another factor that promotes the development of a hiatal hernia is shallow breathing: breathing only into the chest. When the main effort is not done by the diaphragm but by the intercostal muscles, the chest goes up and the sides come in, creating a vacuum effect that sucks the stomach in toward the chest. Teaching your student to breathe properly is very helpful. Ask him to lower the shoulders

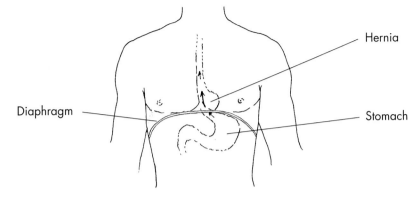

Fig. 6.7. Hiatal hernia

and breathe into the bowl of the belly, allowing the breath to expand the ribs in all directions, like an umbrella. (See The Importance of Breathing Properly in chapter 2.)

Procedure

1. Open the wind gates, the navel, and the pakua as explained in Opening the Wind Gates in chapter 4.
2. Massage the abdomen, releasing the knots and tangles in the stomach and intestines. (For a detailed description of this procedure, refer to *Chi Nei Tsang*.) Emphasize the work on the left corner of the transverse and descending colon, which is located right below the stomach (see "splenic flexure" in fig. 4.10).
3. Spiral and release the wind through the legs and through the arms.

Doing the spleen's, heart's, and lungs' sounds will greatly help to release the pressure and pain, and the liver's sound helps the gallbladder to create bile to aid the digestive process. In addition, your student should keep an alkaline diet, avoiding acidic foods (see chapter 1, "Winds Generated by Food"), and eat small meals, early enough so that the stomach will be empty when he goes to bed and when he needs to make a physical effort. Certain foods might aggravate the condition, and these should be avoided, as should spicy foods and foods that are difficult to digest or high in cholesterol. It is important to chew food well and mix it with saliva and air so that it is easier for the body to digest. It is also important to keep the intestines in prime shape by, for example, eating fiber, and using colonic treatments. Smoking and drinking alcohol, coffee, and carbonated drinks are detrimental for this condition.

A PERSONAL EXPERIENCE I WILL NOT FORGET

I was assisting my master and it was the end of a long day's work. We were about to close up and I'd brought the car around, when a distraught family arrived carrying the grandfather. They had been turned away from different hospitals' emergency rooms. (Some local hospitals would turn away extreme cases so as not to add to their "died in hospital" list.) This was a desperate case—but my master was exhausted after the day's work. He examined the gentleman and raised his eyes to mine. "You want to take care of him?" I replied in the affirmative but told him directly that I didn't know what to do. He responded just as directly, "I'll guide you."

We set to the task by tying his arms down and placing a ball of yarn between his teeth. I began working on the midline between the navel and the solar plexus. His heart constrictor point was like a taut cord; I'd never felt anything that tight in an abdomen. He fainted often, but I continued working with my elbow. After three hours of intense work he stood up, smiled, and walked home with his family. I was nearly drained of energy for three days.

I frequently repeat this story to remind the students of the importance of learning the technique and developing the power to maintain the structure. Sometimes, we must persist for a long time to release the tension and untangle the knots.

Learn. Practice. Persist.

Appendix 1
Chi Nei Tsang Points

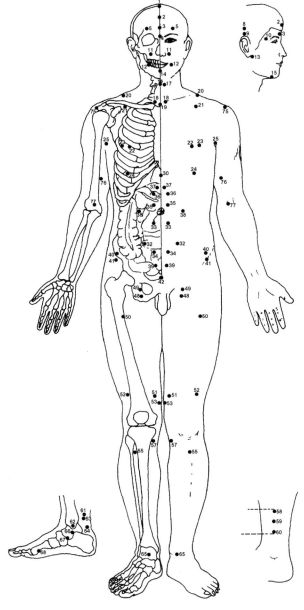

Fig. App. 1.1. Anterior Chi Nei Tsang points

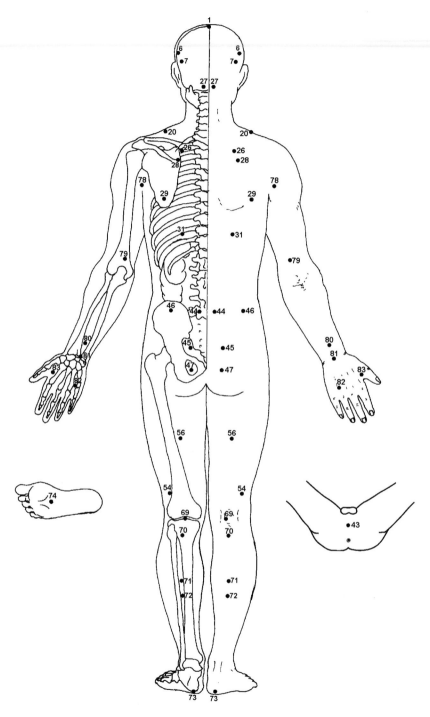

Fig. App. 1.2. Posterior Chi Nei Tsang points

Please Note: The acupuncture point locations referenced in this table are the point locations used by the Universal Tao System. They may differ slightly from point locations found in other texts.

☐ = Not an acupuncture point
GB = Gall Bladder meridian
GV = Governor Vessel
M-HN, M-UE, M-CA, M-BW, M-LE = Miscellaneous points
TW = Triple Warmer

LI = Large intestine
SI = Small intestine
ST = Stomach
SP = Spleen
LU = Lung

KD = Kidney
CV = Conception Vessel
PC = Pericardium
LV = Liver
UB = Urinary bladder

CNT Points	Acupuncture Name	Chinese Name	Location	Traditional Use	Winds
CNT 1	Bai Hui GV 20	Hundred Meeting	On top of the head, at the intersection of lines drawn from the tip of one ear to the other and from the tip of the nose to the back of the head	Clears the senses, calms the spirit, extinguishes the liver wind, stabilizes ascending yang, clears headaches, shock, dizziness, hypertension, insomnia, seizures, prolapsed anus, nasal congestion, stroke, locked jaw, madness, prolapsed uterus, hemorrhoids	5
CNT 2	GV 22		Between CNT 1 and 3, above the hairline		2
CNT 3	Ezhong M-HN 2	Forehead's Middle	In the center of the forehead above the third eye	Sinusitis, insomnia, palpitations, vertigo	2
CNT 4	Yintang M-HN 3	Seal Hall	At the midpoint between the eyebrows	Eliminates wind heat, calms the spirit, headaches, vertigo, colds, hypertension, insomnia, nasal problems, sore eyes, unconsciousness due to loss of blood in childbirth	2
CNT 5	Yangbai GB 14	Yang White	Above the middle of the eyebrow, on a line directly above the pupil of the eye, in the depression of the bone	Eliminates wind, clears the vision, facial paralysis, eye problems, headaches, vomiting, chills, stiff neck	2
CNT 6	Tianchong GB 9	Heaven's Pouring	Above the ear toward the back of the head	Clears headaches, seizures	

CNT Points	Acupuncture Name	Chinese Name	Location	Traditional Use	Winds
CNT 7	Fubai GB 10	Floating White	Above the ears below CNT 6 and farther toward the center of the back of the head	Headache, toothache, deafness, bronchitis	
CNT 8	Jiaosun TW 20	Angle of Regeneration	Above the tip of the ear and natural hairline	Toothache, swollen ears, headache	2, 3
CNT 9			Above the ears directly below point CNT 8 on the hairline	Clears headache	2
CNT 10	Taiyang M-HN 9	The Sun	At the temple, level with the tip of the eyebrows	Disperses winds in the head, cools and clears the eyes, headache, migraine	2
CNT 11	Yingxiang LI 20	Welcome Fragrance	To the sides of the nostrils	Clears the nasal passages, disperses hot wind conditions and facial paralysis	
CNT 12	Dicang ST 4	Earth Granary	On the corners of the mouth	Facial paralysis, drooling	
CNT 13			Below the ears, toward the end of the jawbone Between acupuncture points GB 2 and ST 6.		2, 6, 7
CNT 14	Chengjiang CV 24	Contain Fluid	On the chin, in the depression below the middle of the lower lip	Facial paralysis, toothache, mouth problems, excessive salivation	
CNT 15			In the depression under the chin		
CNT 16	Lianquan CV 23	Modesty's Spring	On the throat, in the depression of the pharyngeal prominence	Bronchitis, pharyngitis, tonsillitis, loss of voice	2, 6
CNT 17	Hongyin M-HN 23	Huge Sound	On the throat to the sides of CNT 16		10
CNT 18			To the sides of CNT 19 on the "V" space between the clavicles		10
CNT 19	Tiantu CV 22	Heaven's Prominence	In the "V" depression between the clavicles	Helps move lung chi, cools the throat, clears the voice	10
CNT 20	Juanjing GB 21	Shoulder Well	Above the clavicle on the shoulder, close to the neck	Stiff neck, coughing	4, 10, 11

CNT Points	Acupuncture Name	Chinese Name	Location	Traditional Use	Winds
CNT 21	Zongfu LU 1	Central Residence	Below the clavicle, toward the joint of the arms	Bronchitis, pneumonia, asthma, tuberculosis, coughing, wheezing, throat blockages, congested nose, sweating, tumors of the neck	4
CNT 22			Above the nipple		1, 9
CNT 23	Tianchi PC 1	Heaven's Pool	Slightly above and on the sides of the nipples, toward the arm	Pain and swelling below the armpits, chest pain	1
CNT 24	Zuoyi or Youyi LV 14	Right and Left Propriety	Between the sixth and seventh ribs in line with the nipple		
CNT 25	Yeling M-UE 40		Inside the armpit		4, 10
CNT 26	Jianwaishu SI 14	Shoulder's Outer Hollow	On the back in the inner side of the scapula, at the level of the second thoracic vertebra	Soreness and pain on the back shoulders	
CNT 27	GV 20	Wind Pond	On the back of the head at the base of the skull above the hairline		2
CNT 28	Fufen B 36	Appended Part	On the back to the inner side of the scapula, at the level of the third thoracic vertebra	Soreness and pain of the shoulders and back	
CNT 29			On the back, toward the lower end of the scapula		
CNT 30	Juque CV 14	Great Palace	Below the lower end of the sternum	Heart reflex point	1, 8, 11, 12
CNT 31	Hunmen B 42	Soul's Door	On the back, toward the sides of the spine at the level of the ninth thoracic vertebra	Liver and gallbladder problems, stomach ache	
CNT 32	Jingzhong M-CA 11	Middle Channel	Below CNT 33, toward the sides of the body	Small intestine reflex point, irregular menstruation, urine retention	1, 3, 8, 11
CNT 33			On a tendon on the navel area at the level between the second and third lumbar vertebrae	Psoas muscle reflex point	3, 4, 5, 6, 7, 8, 9, 11, 12
CNT 34			Below CNT 32 toward the center		

CNT Points	Acupuncture Name	Chinese Name	Location	Traditional Use	Winds
CNT 35			On the navel area, in the upper half of the spleen area on the CNT chart	Spleen reflex point	1, 3, 5, 6, 7, 8, 9, 10, 11, 12
CNT 36			Above the navel area, on the lower half of the heart constrictor of the CNT chart, below CNT 37, slightly toward the sides of the body	Pericardium reflex point	3, 5, 6, 7, 9, 10
CNT 37			On the navel area, on the lower half of the heart constrictor area on the CNT chart	Pericardium reflex point	1, 8, 11, 12
CNT 38			On the navel area comprising the upper end of the kidney area on the CNT chart	Kidney reflex point	3, 7, 8, 11
CNT 39	Dahe KD 12	Great Clarity	On the lower abdomen above the organs		
CNT 40	Wushu GB 27	Five Pivots	On the front, toward the hip bone	Low back pain, bloody vaginal discharges, abdominal pain, constipation	4, 9
CNT 41	Weidao GB 28	Maintain the Way	On the lower tip of the hip bone	Constipation	4, 5, 9, 12
CNT 42	Qugu CV 2	Crooked Bone	On the front above the sexual organs on the pubic bone	Irregular menstruation	
CNT 43	Hui Yin CO 1	Perineum	Between the anus and the scrotum or between the anus and the vagina	Irregular menstruation	5
CNT 44	Yaoyangguan GV 3	Lumbar Yang's Hinge	On the back, on both sides of the spine, between the fourth and fifth lumbar vertebrae	Regulates kidney chi; benefits the lower back and knees	
CNT 45	Baihuanshu B 30	White Circle's Hollow	On the back, in the space between the sacrum and the hip bone	Back pain, anal problems	4, 11
CNT 46	Yaogen M-BW 27	Lower Back's Root	On the back on the upper part of the hip bone, toward the tip, level with the beginning of the sacrum	Problems of the sacro-iliac joint, problems with the legs	

CNT Points	Acupuncture Name	Chinese Name	Location	Traditional Use	Winds
CNT 47	Pangqiang N-BW 18	Strength	On the back at the lower end of the hip bone	Prolapsed anus and uterus	
CNT 48	Yinlian LI 11	Yin's Modesty	On the groin at the level of the sexual organs, toward the inner thigh	Irregular menstruation, hernia	4
CNT 49	Jimai LI 12	Urgent Pulse	Directly above CNT 48 on the groin, at the level of the sexual organs toward the inner thigh	Prolapsed uterus, hernia pain	9
CNT 50	Biguan S 31	Hip's Hinge	On the front of the leg, at the level of the perineum	Paralysis of the legs, knee arthritis, low back pain	
CNT 51	Xue Hai SP 10	Sea of Blood	Above the knee, toward the inside of the leg	Harmonizes chi, cools heat, irregular menstruation, lack of menstruation, uterine bleeding, dripping urine	
CNT 52	Liangqiu ST 34	Ridge Mound	Above the knee, toward the outside of the leg	Calms the stomach, diarrhea, knee problems	
CNT 53	Zuming M-LE 33	Leg's Brightness	In the inner thigh above the knee, toward the end of the femur bone	Arthritis of the knee	1, 3
CNT 54	Shag Yangkuan N-LE 33	Upper Hinge of Yang	On the back of the leg, toward the outside, just above the knee joint	Paralysis of the lower limbs, arthritis of the knee	
CNT 55	ST 36	Knee's Yang Hinge	On the outside part of the front of the leg below the knee		9
CNT 56	Yinshang N-LE 28	Above Abundance	On the back of the leg, on the upper third of the space between the anus and knee	Headaches, low back pain, sciatica	
CNT 57	Yinglingquan SP 9	Yin Tomb Spring	On the inner part of the leg below the knee joint	Retention of urine, urinary infections, irregular menstruation, impotence, dysentery, knee pain	4, 5
CNT 58	Guangming GB 37	Bright light	On the outside of the leg above the ankle	Regulates the liver, clears vision	
CNT 59	Yangfu GB 38	Yang's Help	Directly below CNT 58	Migraines, arthritis of the knee, paralysis of the leg	

CNT Points	Acupuncture Name	Chinese Name	Location	Traditional Use	Winds
CNT 60	Xuan Zhong GB 39	Suspended Time	Directly below CNT 59	Stiff neck, migraines, knee problems	
CNT 61	Shangxi N-LE -3	Upper Stream	Above the ankle bone on the inside of the leg	For foot turned outward	
CNT 62	Taiyinqiao M-LE 11	Great Yin Heel	On the ankle bone on the inside of the leg	Irregular menstruation, uterine bleeding, infertility in women	
CNT 63	Taixi KD 3	Great Creek	Above the ankle bone on the inner side of the leg, toward the back	Good for the kidneys, cools heat, strengthens the lower back and knee, irregular menstruation, lower back pain, paralysis of the legs, in the soles of the feet	9
CNT 64	Dazhong KD 4	Big Goblet	On the inside of the leg directly behind the ankle bone	Asthma, malaria, hysteria, urine retention, pain in the heel	
CNT 65	Zhongfeng LI 4	Middle Seal	On the front of the upper space in front of the ankle bone	Hepatitis, night emission, low abdominal pain, ankle problems	
CNT 66	Zhaohai KD 6	Shining Sea	Directly below the ankle bone on the inside of the foot	Cools heat, calms the spirit, benefits the throat	4, 5, 9, 10
CNT 67			On the inside of the foot below the ankle bone, toward the front, between acupuncture point Rnagu KD 2 and Zhaohal KD 6		10
CNT 68	Tai Bai SP 3	Most White	On the inside of the foot directly behind the metatarsal bone (the big toe)	Headaches, stomachache, water retention, dysentery, constipation	
CNT 69	Wei Zhong B 54	Commission the Middle	On the back of the leg, on the joint behind the knee	Drains summer heat, lower back and knee pain	4, 6
CNT 70	Heyang B 55	Confluence of Yang	On the back of the leg directly below the crease of the knee joint and CNT 69	Soreness from lower back to knee, abnormal uterine bleeding	

CNT Points	Acupuncture Name	Chinese Name	Location	Traditional Use	Winds
CNT 71	Chengjian N-LE-12	Between Supports	On the back of the leg, midway between the back of the knee joint and the heel		
CNT 72	Chengshan B 57	Support the Mountain	On the back of the leg, below point CNT 71	Regulates chi in the yang organs, good for hemorrhoids	
CNT 73			On the heel of the foot right at the tip of the heel bone		
CNT 74	Yongquan KD 1	Bubbling Spring	On the sole of the foot, at a point ⅓ of the distance from the base of the second toe to the heel	Calms the spirit, shock, heat exhaustion, insomnia, stroke, hypertension, mental illness, paralysis of the legs	7, 10, 12
CNT 75	Jian Yu LI 15	Shoulder Bone	On the outer edge of the shoulder, in the depression in the middle of the deltoid muscle	Hypertension, shoulder pain, excessive sweating	4, 11
CNT 76	Gongzhong N-UE 9	Middle of Humerus	In the arm, in the middle of the biceps muscle	Paralysis of the arms, inability to raise the arm, heart palpitations	
CNT 77	Quze PE-3	Crooked Marsh	On the inner side of the arm, just above the joint on the center of the bone	Intestinal problems, bronchitis, heat exhaustion, pain in the elbow and arm	4
CNT 78	Jianzhen SI 9	Shoulder Chastity	On the back, right above the crease of the armpit	Shoulder problems, paralysis of the upper arm, excessive perspiration in the armpits	
CNT 79	Tianjing TW 10	Heaven's Well	On the back of the forearm, in the depression right above the elbow	Elbow problems, migraine, headache, tonsillitis	
CNT 80	Waiguan TW 5	Outer Gate	On the back of the arm just above the wrist	Moves stagnant chi	
CNT 81	Yang Chi TW 4	Pool of Yang	On the back of the arm, in a hollow on the wrist	Relaxes the sinews, clears the channels, relieves heat	
CNT 82	Zhong Zhu TW 3	Middle Island	On the back of the hand, in a hollow between the pinky and ring fingers	Facilitates chi circulation	
CNT 83	Hegu LI 4	Adjoining Valleys	In the back of the hand, in a hollow between the thumb and index fingers	Suppresses pain, clears channels, energizes the lungs	

CHI NEI TSANG POINTS BY ANATOMICAL AREAS

1. Top of the head to eyes: 1 to 10
2. Eyes to mouth: 11 to 13
3. Mouth to neck: 14 to 20
4. Clavicles to sternum (front): 21 to 25
5. Back shoulders to kidneys: 26 to 29
6. Sternum to navel: 30
7. Kidneys to Ming Men: 31
8. Navel: 32 to 38
9. Below navel to sex organs (front and back): 39 to 47
10. Sex organs to knees: 48 to 56
11. Knees to feet: 57 to 74
12. Arms to shoulders to wrists: 75 to 80
13. Wrist to hands: 81 to 83

POINTS FOR EACH WIND

The following are the points used for each wind in the order to be followed. In general, unless otherwise specified, the points in the navel are pressed with the elbow and the related points in the head or limbs are pressed with the knuckles.

1. The First Wind: Wind that Attacks the Liver, the Pericardium, and the Heart
   35L, 35R, 32L, 32R, 37R, 37L, 30, 22, 23, and 53.
2. The Second Wind: Wind that Attacks the Tongue, Jaw, Eyes, and Head
   35L, 35R, 32L, 32R, 37R, 37L, 15, 13, 2, 3, 4, 5, 10, 8, 9, and 27.
3. The Third Wind: Wind that Attacks the Kidneys
   35L, 33L, 33R, 35R, 38L, 32L, 32R, 38R, 36R, 36L, 8, and 53.
4. The Fourth Wind: Wind that Causes Aches, Tightness, Tiredness,

and Uneasiness in the Whole Body and Attacks the Vena Cava, Aorta, and Lumbar Plexus

32L, 32R, 41R, 40R, 40L, 41L, 48L, 48R, 21, 20, 75, 25, 77, 69, 55, 66, and 45.

5. The Fifth Wind: Wind that Makes the Abdomen Stiff, Hard, Tight, and Tender

   35L, 33L, 33R, 35R, 36R, 36L, 41L, 41R, 1, 43, 57, and 66.

6. The Sixth Wind: Wind that Causes Cramps

   35L, 33L, 33R, 35R, 36R, 36L, 15, 13, and 69.

7. The Seventh Wind: Wind that Attacks the Heart Causing Shaking

   35L, 33L, 33R, 35R, 38L, 38R, 36R, 36L, 13, and 74.

8. The Eighth Wind: Wind that Causes Chest Pain

   35L, 33L, 33R, 35R, 38L, 32L, 32R, 38R, 37R, 37L, and 30.

9. The Ninth Wind: Wind that Makes the Legs and Feet Tired

   35L, 33L, 33R, 35R, 36R, 36L, 22, 40L, 41L, 49L, 49R, 41R, 40R, 63, 66, and 55.

10. The Tenth Wind: Wind that Causes Pain, Numbness, and Heat

    35L, 35R, 36R, 36L, 19, 18, 17, 20, 25, 66, 67, and 74.

11. The Eleventh Wind: Wind that Affects the Nerves and Makes the Back Stiff

    35L, 33L, 33R, 35R, 38L, 32L, 32R, 38R, 37R, 37L, 30, 75, 20, and 45.

12. The Twelfth Wind: Wind that Causes Excess Heat and Cold

    35L, 33L, 33R, 35R, 38L, 32L, 32R, 38R, 37R, 37L, 30, 41L, 41R, and 74.

Appendix 2
Practices That Support Chi Nei Tsang

PRACTICING THE SIX HEALING SOUNDS

The Six Healing Sounds will help you sense the distinctive frequencies and colors generated by each organ. Practice the Healing Sounds until you can easily relate the sound to the organ and sense the qualities of that organ.

The Six Healing Sounds Initiate Healing

Everyone has heard stories about gifted beings who possess special healing powers. People seek out great healers. How much time can a great healer spend with you—one hour a week or one hour every day? What about the rest of the week or the rest of the day? One hour a day means one hour out of twenty-four. One hour a week means one out of 168 hours. This is why it is important for each person to learn how to clear her own negative energy, and how to transform it into good energy. Regular practice of self-maintenance and self-healing enhances ongoing healing. The Six Healing Sounds are an easy practice to initiate healing. The sounds are very simple, but very powerful.

When you are adept at the Six Healing Sounds and begin to practice Chi Nei Tsang, you will need to teach your students the sounds.

They can practice at home and help carry on the healing. You should teach one or two sounds at each session, and review them at the next session.

How to Make the Six Healing Sounds

The Lungs' Sound

Associated organ: Large intestine
Element: Metal
Season: Autumn
Color: White
Negative Emotions: Grief, sadness, depression, sorrow
Positive Emotions: Courage, righteousness, justice, detachment
Sound: Sss-s-s-s-s-s (tongue behind teeth)

1. **Position:** Sit with your back straight and the backs of your hands resting on your thighs. Smile down to your lungs. Take a deep breath and raise your arms out in front of you. When the hands are at eye level, begin to rotate the palms, bringing them above your head until they are palms up, pushing upward. Point the fingers toward those of the opposite hand. Keep the elbows rounded out to the sides. Do not straighten your arms.

2. **Sound:** Close your jaw so that the teeth gently meet, and part your lips slightly. Inhale as you look up, eyes wide open, and push your palms upward and out as you slowly exhale through your teeth and make the sound "sss-s-s-s-s-s." At first you can produce the lungs' sound aloud, but eventually you should practice subvocally (vocalizing so softly that only you can hear the sound). Picture and feel excess heat, sick energy, sadness, sorrow, depression, and grief expelled as the sacs surrounding the lungs compress. Exhale slowly and fully.

3. **Rest and Concentrate:** Resting is very important because during rest you can communicate with your inner self and your internal system. When you have exhaled completely, rotate the palms down

as you slowly lower the shoulders, and return your hands to your lap, palms up. Close your eyes and be aware of your lungs. Smile into them and imagine that you are still making the lungs' sound. Breathe normally and picture your lungs growing with a bright white color. This will strengthen your lungs and draw down the universal energy associated with them. With each breath, try to feel the exchange of cool, fresh energy as it replaces excessively hot energy. Repeat 3, 6, 9, 12, or 24 times. Practice more often to alleviate sadness, depression, colds, flu, toothaches, asthma, and emphysema.

The Kidneys' Sound

Associated organ: Urinary bladder
Element: Water
Season: Winter
Color: Blue or black
Negative Emotions: Fear, shock
Positive Emotions: Gentleness, stillness, alertness, gratitude
Sound: Choo-oo-oo-oo (as when blowing out a candle with the lips forming an "O")

1. **Position:** Bring your legs together, ankles and knees touching. Be aware of your kidneys and smile into them. Take a deep breath, lean forward, and clasp the fingers of both hands together around your knees. Pull your arms straight from the lower back while bending the torso forward (this allows your back to protrude in the area of the kidneys). Simultaneously tilt your head upward as you look straight ahead and maintain the pull on your arms from the lower back. Feel your spine pull.

2. **Sound:** Round the lips and slightly exhale the sound "choo-oo-oo-oo" as if you were blowing out a candle. Simultaneously contract your abdomen, pulling it in toward your kidneys. Imagine the excess heat, fear, and wet, sick energies squeezed out from the fasciae surrounding them.

3. **Rest and Concentrate:** After you have fully exhaled, sit erect, separate the legs, and place your hands on your thighs, palms up. Close your eyes, breathe into the kidneys, and be aware of them. Picture the bright color blue in the kidneys. Smile into them, imagining that you are still making the kidneys' sound. Repeat the above steps 3, 6, 12, or 24 times. Practice more often to alleviate fear, fatigue, dizziness, ringing in the ears, or back pain.

❧ The Liver's Sound

Associated Organ: Gallbladder
Element: Wood
Season: Spring
Color: Green
Negative Emotions: Anger, aggression
Positive Emotions: Kindness, generosity, forgiveness, self-expansion, identity
Sound: Sh-h-h-h-h-h-h (tongue near palate)

1. **Position:** Sit comfortably and straight. Be aware of the liver and smile into it. When you feel you are in touch with the liver, extend your arms out to your sides, palms up. Take a deep breath as you slowly raise the arms up and over the head from the sides, following this action with your eyes. Interlace the fingers and turn your joined hands over to face the ceiling, palms up. Push out at the heel of the palms and stretch the arms out from the shoulders. Bend slightly to the left, exerting a gentle pull on the liver.

2. **Sound:** Open your eyes wide because they are the openings of the liver. Slowly exhale the sound "sh-h-h-h-h-h-h" subvocally. Envision expelling excess heat and anger from the liver, as the fasciae around it compresses.

3. **Rest and Concentrate:** When you have fully exhaled, separate the hands, turn the palms down, and slowly bring the arms down to your sides, leading with the heels of the hands. Bring the hands to rest on your thighs, palms up. Smile down into the liver. Close

your eyes, breathe into it, and imagine you are still making the liver's sound. Repeat 3, 6, 12, or 24 times. Practice more often to alleviate red or watery eyes, to remove a sour or bitter taste, and to detoxify the liver.

The Heart's Sound

Associated organ: Small intestine
Element: Fire
Season: Summer
Color: Red
Negative Emotions: Impatience, arrogance, hastiness, cruelty, violence
Positive Emotions: Joy, happiness, honor, sincerity, creativity, enthusiam
Sound: Haw-w-w-w-w-w (mouth wide open)

1. **Position:** Be aware of your heart and smile into it. Take a deep breath and assume the same position as for the liver's sound. Unlike the former exercise, however, you will lean slightly to the right to pull gently against the heart, which is just to the left of the center of your chest. Focus on your heart, and feel the tongue's connection to it.

2. **Sound:** Open your mouth, round your lips, and slowly exhale the sound "haw-w-w-w-w-w" subvocally. Picture the sac around the heart expelling heat, impatience, hastiness, arrogance, and cruelty.

3. **Rest and Concentrate:** After having exhaled, smile into your heart, and picture a bright red color. Repeat the steps above 3 to 24 times. Practice more often to relieve sore throats, cold sores, swollen gums or tongue, jumpiness, moodiness, and heart disease.

The Spleen's Sound

Associated organs: Pancreas, stomach
Element: Earth
Season: Indian summer

Color: Yellow
Negative Emotions: Worry, anxiety, pity
Positive Emotions: Fairness, openess, compassion, centering, balance
Sound: Who-o-o-o-o-o (from the throat, guttural)

1. **Position:** Be aware of the spleen and smile into it. Take a deep breath as you place the fingers of both hands just beneath the sternum on the left side. You will press in with your fingers as you push your middle back outward.

2. **Sound:** Look out, and gently push your fingertips into the left of the solar plexus area, as you sub-vocally exhale the sound "Who-o-o-o-o-o" This is more guttural, or "throaty" than the kidneys' sound. Unlike blowing out a candle, this sound originates from the depths of the throat rather than from the mouth. Feel the spleen's sound vibrate the vocal cords. Feel any worries being transformed as the virtues of fairness and compassion arise.

3. **Rest and Concentrate:** Once you have fully exhaled, close your eyes, place the hands on the thighs, palms up, and concentrate smiling energy on your spleen, pancreas, and stomach. Breathe into these organs as you picture a bright yellow light shining in your organs. Repeat the steps above 3 to 24 times. Practice more often to eliminate indigestion, nausea, and diarrhea.

The Triple Warmer's Sound

The Triple Warmer refers to the three energy centers of the body: The upper section (brain, heart, and lungs) is hot; the middle section (liver, kidneys, stomach, pancreas, and spleen) is warm; and the lower section (large and small intestines, bladder, and sexual organs) is cool. The sound "hee-e-e-e-e-e" balances the temperature of the three levels by bringing hot energy down to the lower center and cold energy up to the higher centers. Specifically, hot energy from the area of the heart moves to the colder sexual region, and cold energy from the lower abdomen is moved up to the heart's region.

1. **Position:** Lie on your back with your arms resting palms up at your sides, and keep your eyes closed. Inhale fully into all three cavities: chest, solar plexus, and lower abdomen.

2. **Sound:** Exhale the sound "hee-e-e-e-e-e" subvocally, first flattening your chest, then your solar plexus, and finally your lower abdomen. Imagine a large roller pressing out your breath as it moves from your head down to your sexual center.

3. **Rest and Concentrate:** When you have fully exhaled, concentrate on the entire body. Repeat the above steps from 3 to 24 times. Practice more often to relieve insomnia and stress.

Daily Practice before Bedtime

Practice the Six Healing Sounds before going to bed at night. This will help calm the body, promote good sleep, and cool down any overheated organs. Before you go to sleep, clear the negative emotions so that the positive emotions can grow. Clearing out the negative emotions will chase away nightmares. You can sleep well and connect to the universal mind to recharge your energy.

If you have problems or feel ill, attain the sensation of emptiness and send these disturbances up into the universal mind. Trust that this force will help you. In the morning, smile inwardly and see for yourself when you awake.

The Six Healing Sounds and Inner Smile practices are more fully explained and illustrated in *The Six Healing Sounds: Taoist Techniques for Balancing Chi* (Rochester, Vt.: Destiny Books, 2009) and *The Inner Smile: Increasing Chi through the Cultivation of Joy* (Rochester, Vt.: Destiny Books, 2008).

FANNING AND VENTING SICK ENERGY

These exercises are particularly good for the Chi Nei Tsang practitioner to practice daily to get rid of sick energy and negative emotions so that positive emotions can grow and circulate. They can also drain the excess heat from a student, but the student must practice regularly at home to receive their full benefit.

Fanning

Since tension causes a lot of sick, negative emotional energy to condense in the chest, the heart can easily become jammed. Some believe that long-term negative emotions such as hatred, impatience, and arrogance directly affect heart conditions or are a major cause of heart attacks. To protect yourself, you can activate the heart. This process will draw the negative feelings and sick energy to the heart. You will need to fan this energy out of the heart and body.

Taoists regard the soles of the feet and centers of the palms as having a connection with the heart. Therefore, fanning sick energy involves moving the energy from the heart down to the soles of the feet (fig. App. 2.1). The theory is that when you fan the sick energy down to the soles of the feet and further down to the earth, the soles

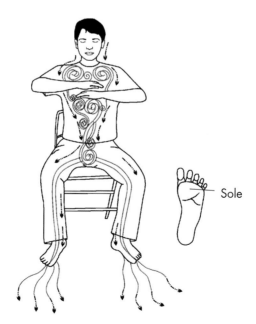

Fig. App. 2.1. Fanning the sick energy and negative emotions from the heart to the soles of the feet

connect with Mother Earth, who can accept the sick and negative energy to utilize and transform it into useful energy. In contrast, if a person expresses the negative energy as emotions and "dumps" it from the higher place of the heart, it will not be received by Mother Earth who can put it to good use. Instead, these emotions will be received by other people involved in the person's life, a situation that can cause sickness for them as well.

Position and Practice for Fanning

This can be done standing or sitting. Fanning is an activity originating in the upper diaphragm and in the mind. With the palm facing downward, raise the left hand to the chest at the level of the heart center, about 1½ inches from the top of the sternum. Place the right hand parallel and above it.

1. Practice the heart's sound (haw-w-w-w-w-w) and feel the heat from the heart start to burn, drawing in any negative feelings.
2. Exhale this energy (using the heart's sound) as you simultaneously lower both hands. Feel the negative energies burn out. Continue to exhale the energy down to the perineum, both feet, to the soles, and then perceive Mother Earth absorbing it. Rest the palms on the knees. Look down to the soles of the feet and feel a cloudy, grey, and cold or chilly energy go out. Rest again. Be sure to take a long time to rest since your resting time is very important.
3. Start over again by returning both hands to the heart level. Practice 18 to 36 times for a total of 5 to 10 minutes. As you clear yourself of the dirty, sick energy, you will feel empty, but in a good mood. Feel the heavenly energy as a golden light coming down through the head and filling the body.
4. Rest for a while. You also will feel Mother Earth's energy, a blue color, coming up through the soles of your feet.

Venting

When negative emotions are causing sickness in the organs, venting is another practice to remove the undesirable energy. For example, fear in the kidneys can be vented to change the color of their energy from a cloudy blue energy to a bright blue. Anger produces cloudiness in the liver's color, which can be changed from a cloudy green back to a bright, clear green.

 ## Position and Practice for Venting

After you finish the Fanning practice as above, remain in the same sitting position to begin the Venting exercise. Venting gets rid of emotions from all the other organs. Since fingers and toes are connected with all the organs and glands (fig. App. 2.2), sick energy tends to stagnate there, making them feel numb.

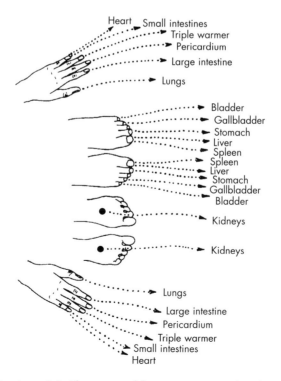

Fig. App. 2.2. The toes and fingers correspond to the organs.

1. Sit and place your hands on your knees. Keep your fingers slightly spread apart and pointed toward the toes.

2. Place your feet parallel to each other and point the toes up. Be aware of the area 2 or 3 inches up and directly between the big toes. Be aware of the tips of the big toes and then all of the toes.

3. If you have sick energy affecting an organ, look at figure App. 2.2 to determine the toes or fingers that correspond to that organ. While venting, you can emphasize the fingers or toes corresponding to the organ in which you have the sick energy to send more of the energy out of the body. For example, if you have a heart problem, you can concentrate on the pinky fingers. Feel the cloudy gray energy exiting through those fingers.

4. Practice the triple warmer's sound (hee-e-e-e-e-e) down to the navel, perineum, and toes (figures App. 2.3 and App. 2.4). With

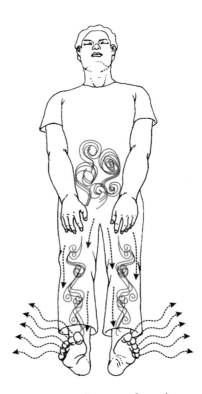

Fig. App. 2.3. Venting sick energy from the organs to the lower abdomen and the toes

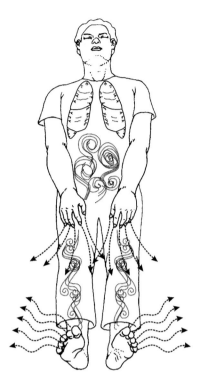

Fig. App. 2.4. Venting sick energy from the diaphragm to the lower abdomen

the hee-e-e-e-e-e sound, feel the vibration of the sound at and moving out of the tips of the fingers and toes.

5. Gradually feel a steaming, dark, cloudy, cold or chilly, sick emotional energy emerging from the toes and fingers.

6. Picture the energy becoming brighter and brighter. Continue to look at the point between the big toes to see more sick energy and negative feelings emerge.

7. Be aware of the liver and see it become a bright green.

8. Be aware of the spleen and the pancreas, and see them glow with a bright yellow color.

9. Be aware of the lungs and see them glow with a white light.

10. Be aware of the heart and see it open with a bright red light.

11. Be aware of the kidneys; see them glow with a bright blue light.

About the Author

Mantak Chia has been studying the Taoist approach to life since childhood. His mastery of this ancient knowledge, enhanced by his study of other disciplines, has resulted in the development of the Universal Tao System, which is now being taught throughout the world.

Mantak Chia was born in Thailand to Chinese parents in 1944. When he was six years old, he learned from Buddhist monks how to sit and "still the mind." While in grammar school he learned traditional Thai boxing, and soon went on to acquire considerable skill in Aikido, Yoga, and Tai Chi. His studies of the Taoist way of life began in earnest when he was a student in Hong Kong, ultimately leading to his mastery of a wide variety of esoteric disciplines, with the guidance of several masters, including Master I Yun, Master Meugi, Master Cheng Yao Lun, and Master Pan Yu. To better understand the mechanisms behind healing energy, he also studied Western anatomy and medical sciences.

Master Chia has taught his system of healing and energizing practices to tens of thousands of students and trained more than two thousand instructors and practitioners throughout the world. He has established centers for Taoist study and training in many countries around the globe. In June of 1990, he was honored by the International Congress of Chinese Medicine and Qi Gong (Chi Kung), which named him the Qi Gong Master of the Year.

The Universal Tao System and Training Center

THE UNIVERSAL TAO SYSTEM

The ultimate goal of Taoist practice is to transcend physical boundaries through the development of the soul and the spirit within the human. That is also the guiding principle behind the Universal Tao, a practical system of self-development that enables individuals to complete the harmonious evolution of their physical, mental, and spiritual bodies. Through a series of ancient Chinese meditative and internal energy exercises, the practitioner learns to increase physical energy, release tension, improve health, practice self-defense, and gain the ability to heal him- or herself and others. In the process of creating a solid foundation of health and well-being in the physical body, the practitioner also creates the basis for developing his or her spiritual potential by learning to tap into the natural energies of the sun, moon, earth, stars, and other environmental forces.

The Universal Tao practices are derived from ancient techniques rooted in the processes of nature. They have been gathered and integrated into a coherent, accessible system for well-being that works directly with the life force, or chi, that flows through the meridian system of the body.

Master Chia has spent years developing and perfecting techniques for teaching these traditional practices to students around the world through ongoing classes, workshops, private instruction, and healing sessions, as well as books and video and audio products. Further information can be obtained at www.universal-tao.com.

THE UNIVERSAL TAO TRAINING CENTER

The Tao Garden Resort and Training Center in northern Thailand is the home of Master Chia and serves as the worldwide headquarters for Universal Tao activities. This integrated wellness, holistic health, and training center is situated on eighty acres surrounded by the beautiful Himalayan foothills near the historic walled city of Chiang Mai. The serene setting includes flower and herb gardens ideal for meditation, open-air pavilions for practicing Chi Kung, and a health and fitness spa.

The center offers classes year round, as well as summer and winter retreats. It can accommodate two hundred students, and group leasing can be arranged. For information worldwide on courses, books, products, and other resources, see below.

RESOURCES

Universal Healing Tao Center
274 Moo 7, Luang Nua, Doi Saket, Chiang Mai, 50220 Thailand
Tel: (66)(53) 495-596 Fax: (66)(53) 495-852
E-mail: universaltao@universal-tao.com
Website: www.universal-tao.com

For information on retreats and the health spa, contact:
Tao Garden Health Spa & Resort
E-mail: info@tao-garden.com, taogarden@hotmail.com
Website: www.tao-garden.com

Good Chi • Good Heart • Good Intention

Index

Page numbers in *italics* refer to illustrations.

BOOKS OF RELATED INTEREST

Chi Nei Tsang
Chi Massage for the Vital Organs
by Mantak Chia

Healing Light of the Tao
Foundational Practices to Awaken Chi Energy
by Mantak Chia

Chi Self-Massage
The Taoist Way of Rejuvenation
by Mantak Chia

Bone Marrow Nei Kung
Taoist Techniques for Rejuvenating the Blood and Bone
by Mantak Chia

Wisdom Chi Kung
Practices for Enlivening the Brain with Chi Energy
by Mantak Chia

The Inner Smile
Increasing Chi through the Cultivation of Joy
by Mantak Chia

The Taoist Soul Body
Harnessing the Power of Kan and Li
by Mantak Chia

The Secret Teachings of the Tao Te Ching
by Mantak Chia and Tao Huang

INNER TRADITIONS • BEAR & COMPANY
P.O. Box 388
Rochester, VT 05767
1-800-246-8648
www.InnerTraditions.com

Or contact your local bookseller